STRAIGHTEN YOUR

NAVIGATING LIFE'S CHALLENGES WITH GRACE

DEBBIE ADAMS

Quantity sales and special discounts are available on quantity purchases by corporations, associations, and others. For details, contact the publisher at the address above.

Orders by U.S. trade bookstores and wholesalers. Email info@ BeyondPublishing.net

The Beyond Publishing Speakers Bureau can bring authors to your live event. For more information or to book an event contact the Beyond Publishing Speakers Bureau speak@BeyondPublishing.net

The Author can be reached directly at BeyondPublishing.net

Manufactured and printed in the United States of America distributed globally by BeyondPublishing.net

BEYOND
PUBLISHING

New York | Los Angeles | London | Sydney

ISBN Softcover: 978-1-63792-675-8
ISBN Hardcover: 978-1-63792-674-1

I want to say a heart felt THANK YOU to my friend Stella for offering to paint a picture for my book cover and the picture you painted is truly a reflection of what God put in my mind.

I also want to say THANK YOU to all my friends and family for all of their support and encouragement as I wrote this book and sought God's direction.

Table of Contents

Introduction

Life gives us all kinds of ups and downs. Sometimes our life is great and at other times, we go through struggles. No matter what those situations in our life journey may be, don't let them knock you down and get you to going the wrong direction. Keep your crown on straight and keep looking up to God. Let God be your stronghold in life and the One you turn to when your life journey gets complicated.

Those of us who know Jesus have a Crown that we carry and it's not on our head for others to see.......it's in our heart and soul where only God can see. Others can see our crown through our testimony. We hear of crowns and think of a King or Queen in England where the Royalty is or so we think. This world would have you to think that there's royalty in this world; however True Royalty is with our Lord and Savior. When the Royalty in England is finished in this life, their crowns will only be shown on this earth for the world to see and hopefully it wasn't just for the world, and they did have the TRUE CROWN of Jesus in their heart and soul.

My friends, let's all concentrate on our crown and its location and whether we're just showing off our crown in this world for others to see or whether it's in our hearts and souls. If you have your crown only for others to see, then you're making it easily accessible for others to knock it down. You want to always have your Crown straight and you don't want to always be trying to straighten it. If it's just for a show, then you will be continuing to straighten it every day; however, if you have it in your heart and soul, you will have Jesus helping you to keep it straight. Just remember that in this world we are just passing through to a better home in Heaven. Think of it like a vacation when you go to a different state or country for a brief time and then you go home. That's exactly what we who have Jesus in our hearts are doing in this world we live in. This world may get crazy at times; however, God is always here with us in our hearts and souls helping us along our life journey.

We all see the beauty in a Crown and our life is beautiful too no matter what is happening because God is always there. Whether you're on the mountain top or in the valley, God is always there with you. ALWAYS REMEMBER THAT!! I was in the valley for about 2 years straight and God never left my side. Those of you who think you can do life better on your own (and believe me you can't) remember God's plans are always better than ours no matter the situation. Believe me, I've tried doing it on my own and God's plans are always better. When life is going good, God is there and when we think life is bad, God is still there. Life never is bad, but we seem to think certain situations in our life make it bad; however, God knows it's not bad and it's the sin and evil in this world that makes it bad. Our life can be bad and ugly simply because we don't turn to God for help. God is our navigator in this life and that's like a tour guide and God will never send you down the wrong road. It's us that go down the wrong path simply by our choices in life and all choices that we make have consequences that are either good or bad depending on what we choose. I'm sure you have heard the saying that they brought that on themselves, meaning that if they hadn't chosen to go down that path, then their life journey would have been different. We will all struggle in this life and some more than others and we need to call out to God and ask for His help and He will make our struggles a little easier. Matthew 11:28-30 says "Come unto me, all ye that labour and are heavy laden, and I will give you rest. Take my yoke upon you and learn of me; for I am meek and lowly in heart: and ye shall find rest unto your souls. For my yoke is easy, and my burden is light." Let Jesus Christ carry your burden and make your load lighter.

Straighten your crown and let Jesus take the wheel as that country song says and let Him take control of your life. If you're a Child of the King, you're wearing a crown because you have the Holy Spirit in your soul. No matter what is going on in your life, remember that with God, life is always beautiful because God makes everything beautiful even during heartbreak and despair. So don't let this world make you see ugly when there is beauty all around. Open your eyes and straighten your crown and let God help you to see beauty in everything around you. Whether you're a man, woman, boy or girl, you're a Child of the King if you know Jesus and have Him in your heart. As a Child of the King, we have a crown to wear, and that crown shows your royalty with our Lord and Savior Jesus Christ. Keep your crown straight so others may see your testimony and they can see that your confidence comes from God. Your confidence should only come from the one and only Lord Jesus Christ who leads and guides your way every single day and every hour and minute and second of your day. Why do you let troubles in this cruel world bother you? Turn it over to God and let Him take care of what is bothering you and let God give you the peace over your struggles. Life is all about decisions and those decisions make you who you are. Let God be the One who guides you and gives you wisdom to make the correct decisions in your journey of life.

Let's go on this journey together as we explore the Crown that we've been given to wear not on our heads but in our hearts and souls. Let us wear it and make our Heavenly Father happy that we're not letting anything come to defeat us and we're trusting only in Him. We all have a testimony, and our Crown is showing our testimony to others so let us show others our faith and how we can keep our crown straight as we trust only in God to help us through life. Now let's dive in a little deeper and explore all the aspects of this Crown and be proud to be wearing God's Crown in our hearts as we journey through this road of life. Believe me friend, when I say it will only get better! Now let's get ready for our journey of enlightenment as we talk about our Crown in our Heart.

Chapter 1

GRACEFUL COMPOSURE IN CHAOS

∞∞∞

You might be asking how you can have composure during chaos; however, if you're trusting God to guide you, then you can because all things are possible with God. When things go crazy in this world and they will, we need to do a heart check and not sound off with the first attitude that comes to mind. Remember what words you say in the heat of the moment cannot be taken back. After they are spoken, they are out there for the world to hear. If you only spoke them in your heart, only God heard them and He will forgive you if you ask for forgiveness, but whether we spoke them for all to hear or only in our hearts, we need to speak and act with proper attitudes. I'm right there with you because I've done this before when a situation was happening, and I might even have yelled at someone and then I had to ask God for forgiveness because my heart knew that wasn't the proper way to act and my actions were knocking my crown down and so I had to straighten it back up. So, when chaos comes knocking at your door, think before you act as my dad always says and always remember that your testimony is showing the place of your crown. If your crown is straight, then people will see a good testimony by your actions and if your crown needs straightening, then people will most likely see your testimony as one that needs work and repair. Whether you realize it or not, people are watching you and me every day in whatever situation we're in so let's try and have a testimony that shows others that God is the King in our lives. After all, if you truly know Jesus Christ, you are a Child of the King and you're wearing His Crown!

So, we know that we should have a graceful composure in how we handle situations in our lives. What exactly does be graceful mean? We know that God extends His grace to us every day and gives us blessings that we probably don't deserve. For us as humans what does being graceful in chaos mean for us and how we act? Webster says graceful is "marked by tact and delicacy; merciful, compassionate; pleasing in line, proportion, or movement." This sounds like our Lord and how He acts toward us doesn't it. Well, that should tell you that we need to be more Christ like and act as much like Jesus as we possibly can. We are humans and are covered in human skin so we are not perfect like our Lord so it's hard for us to be exactly like Him; however, we can get as close as possible and do things that we know are pleasing to Him. Yes, we will mess up at times and believe me, I've messed up a lot in my life and then I make changes in my life to straighten my crown and go on. So how can we be gracious when we have chaos in our lives and our immediate response is to worry, get aggravated and frustrated and even yell and call people names. A lot of times we need to just take a deep breath and get on the right attitudes, or we will not be displaying the proper testimony and people will see that our crown isn't straight. You might be thinking that people won't see when our crowns are not straight, but they will because our hearts display our crowns. I'm sure you have heard the saying that what you say flows from your heart because what is in your heart will be reflected in the words you say and the attitudes you portray. If your heart isn't right, then what you say, and your actions and attitudes won't be right. So, to display graceful composure during chaos, we need to have a positive attitude, and think and speak with poise and dignity.

I'm always trying to stay positive in whatever situation I'm faced with and sometimes it's hard especially when you're around someone that is a negative person, and they see the bad before the good. I've had to tell negative people before that if they will just look, there is a positive side to the situation. You might be one of those negative people and if you are, I hope that you will see the beauty in our world and start thinking positively. I understand that some situations that we're faced with can be stressful at times and I've had a few of those and stress isn't good for anyone. We need to stay away from stress as much as possible and a good way to do that when you feel like you're about to get stressed is to take a deep breath. I've got a friend that has her own podcast show and at the beginning of every show she will start with breathing exercises for about 7 seconds and end with saying thank you. This is good practice to do even if it's only for 7 seconds and always remember to thank the Lord for everything even the chaos. Have you ever noticed that if you thank the Lord for the situation, that it seems to get better and it doesn't seem as bad as before. God likes for us to say thank you to Him even for the little things and especially for the big things. So, if you're not already doing it, let's start doing it. I made it a practice to be thankful even for the new day God has given me after I was diagnosed with cancer 15 years ago. Thank the Lord I'm cancer free and it's all because of Him. Sometimes you might need to take yourself out of a certain chaos in your life even if it's just for a few minutes or a day because not thinking about a situation can help you more than you realize. You don't think about it or stress over it because you're being distracted while you're doing something else. You might need to go have a fun night with your friends just to get your mind off some situation. Then when you go back to it, your mind will be refreshed, and you can concentrate more on what needs to be done in the situation. We can all manage our lives better with a clear head and sometimes just getting away for a bit can help keep our hearts and Crown on the straight path.

We can be graceful by following the Lord's example so how do we keep our composure in those tough situations we face on our journey of life? Composure is being able to see clearly in a situation without being angry or aggravated because you don't like the situation. It's being calm during chaos. That is hard to do sometimes but you can do it. You need to concentrate on what the situation involves and what needs to be done and ask God to help you. He will help you by giving you wisdom and strength and by keeping you calm and composed during life challenges. It might be a trial you're facing in your life or a situation that arose out of living our life. Whatever the situation, always ask God for His help and either He will take care of the situation, or He will help you to get through the situation. There have been times in my life that I was going through trials, and I couldn't understand why, and I think sometimes God might be testing our faith in Him by the trials and situations we face in life. That's one good reason why we need to go through any chaos in our life with graceful composure because God wants to see that our total faith is in Him and Him alone. He wants to see that we totally trust Him for everything in our lives. Trust in God also involves faith and to have faith, we need to totally trust God. That means trust Him in everything and not to call on Him just in emergencies. I'm sure you've heard the expression of using God as a spare tire. When life is good, we might try to do things on our own and then when we have struggles in our lives, then we will call on God like we're saying ok God help me out of this emergency that arose. He will always be there and will help us and answer our prayers in any situation; however, He likes us to fully depend on and trust in Him and that means in the good times as well as the bad times. If you trust God to help you in emergency situations, why not trust Him in everything? Are we so self-righteous that we think we don't need God in the good times; however, friend, we need God all the time. God sees the future and we can't see what's going to happen tomorrow, but God is already there and knows what we will face. God loves us so much that He suffered on the cruel cross of Calvary to pay for our sins in this world so why not fully trust Him, He knows your needs better than anyone because He is the one who created you and He loves you.

So, to handle life's struggles with grace when we're going through something in our life journey, I hope you're seeing that we need to have God as our pilot and not our copilot. As I mentioned earlier, there was a period of about 2 years that I was in the valley, and I was wondering what was going to happen next. I was fully trusting God to carry me through each situation and to help me and life is much better when we're letting God drive the car and lead us as we're facing challenges on our journey of life. It wasn't that I didn't question and wonder why I was going through the challenges and trials because I did, and I cried out to God to help me to understand and to get me through it all. After those 2 years events of trials and challenges, my faith became stronger, and God was there helping me with what I had to face. Looking back on it now, I can see times when He was carrying me through the storms of my life. Keep your Crown straight and Keep your faith in God and your life won't be perfect; however, our God who is perfect in every way will help you to get through whatever challenge you may face. Our God is mighty and gracious and won't let you face anything more than you're able to bear. You might think that what you're facing is too hard for you to handle; however, God knows the limits to what you can handle more than you and I do, and He will help us to handle what life throws at us. Being gracefully composed while dealing with chaos in our lives isn't as complicated as we make it out to be. God wants you to be able to use your testimony to show others that your Crown is straight and that you face every day with the faith and assurance that whatever you face it will be alright because God is at the helm of the ship, and you trust His leading and His alone to get you through every challenge in your journey of life.

I hope you're beginning to see that graceful composure during chaos is having the right attitude and staying calm and collected during uncertainty. It's the ability to maintain composure without becoming stressed and showing our emotional well-being with grace during chaos and allowing us to make better decisions and have a positive influence on those around us. If we have a positive attitude toward our life challenges, then others will also be influenced as they watch us tackle uncertainties in our life. You will also be able to foster inner strength that only God can give you. God is steering our lives through turbulent waters and He will help you in any uncertainties that you're facing. It's about seeing and acknowledging the challenges in our lives and deciding to remain calm as our Creator gives us strength and clarity of thought and mind in the unpredictability of life's journey. In any challenge we are faced with, God is giving us an opportunity for growth in our faith and for learning. If we're gracious in our composure, we can portray kindness and goodwill and the proper attitude. Being gracious is a divine attribute and a virtuous attribute that we portray simply because we have God helping us to give us clarity in every situation in our lives. There are several ways that we can show graceful composure in dealing with life's challenges.

1. Mindfulness- this is always being mindful about your emotions and keeping your emotions in check. Acknowledge what your emotions and thoughts are and don't get overwhelmed or stressed. Stay focused on the issue at hand and have clarity in your thoughts.

2. Self-Reflection- this is understanding your feelings and how and why you respond to certain situations in a certain way. If you know you respond to certain situations in a bad manner or possibly have a bad attitude, then understand why that is and ask God to help you to have a better response so you may respond more consciously.

3. Perspective- start looking at challenges as new opportunities to learn and grow. Change your perspective on things and you will see how you can have a graceful composure as you attempt challenges in your life.

4. Adaptability- being able to accept change allows you to adapt to life's uncertainty. You will accept life's uncertainty with more flexibility and understanding.

5. Empathy- understand others perspective as well as your own and you will be able to show kindness more freely. Love others as God loves us.

6. Assertiveness- letting your voice be heard. Everyone has boundaries and needs, and you need to feel comfortable sharing with others what these are. This is when others try to run over you in some form or fashion and you need to stand up for yourself.
7. Breathing- we talked about this earlier that you might need to stop and take a deep breath or simply walk away from the situation for a minute or two. This will help you to stay calm and focused on the issue at hand. Walking away and taking a deep breath will give you a clearer picture of the situation.
8. Learn from Adversity- with each challenge in our lives, we're given the opportunity to grow and learn from each one. Each difficulty can be a step towards progress in our lives. Whatever you're faced with, ask God what it is that He wants you to learn.

Any challenge that we face should be handled with faith in God and there are several ways of doing that. First and foremost, we need to pray to God and ask for His guidance and wisdom in how to handle the situations we face in life. God will also give you the strength you need for any situation. You also need to stay focused in God's Word as He will talk to you through His Word if you listen for that still small voice. We must also trust in God's Plans for our life. As we talked about earlier, God's plans for our life are much better than any of our plans. Trusting God will give you comfort as well as guidance because He will show you the way and open and close doors that no man can open or close. Whatever challenge you're facing now, it's always good to ask others to pray for you and your situation and that will encourage you more than you know. Anytime someone tells me they're praying for me, that always helps to encourage me. No matter what is going on in your life, always remember to be grateful and to thank the Lord for all the blessings He has bestowed on your life. Acknowledging how good God is will always help you in so many ways and will give you strength in times of uncertainty. Know your limits in everything you encounter in life and know that God will show you how to tackle challenges that come, and He may even send someone to help you depending on what the situation happens to be. Trusting God for strength and everything you need is much better than trying to do it all on your own. Once we see and understand that challenges are a part of life's journey, we can approach any difficulty and uncertainty with patience and perseverance knowing that growth will most likely arise from our adversity, and we can tackle any challenge with graceful composure. As long as you have God with you as you encounter life's challenges, He will give you strength, comfort, and guidance so you may tackle any uncertainty of life.

Chapter 2

BLOSSOMING THROUGH STRUGGLES

How do you handle the struggles that come into your life? We all have struggles and the way that we handle them can be good or bad. There's no right or wrong way to handle them because certain struggles will affect different people in different ways. Our struggles can either shape us or break us so let your struggles shape you into a better person instead of breaking you down into someone you don't need to be. You don't want to be discouraged over a situation that is happening or has happened in your life. Like I mentioned earlier, always try, and find the positive in everything because everything is beautiful. I've been through a lot of struggles in my own life from cancer, marriage dissolvement, job loss, and death of several family and friends so I can understand how hard it is to find the good when you're going through life struggles; however, it can be done. The only way it can be done is to ask God to help you get through whatever struggle you're facing, and He will help you. He will never leave you or forsake you and He will always be there to help you and will give you strength, wisdom, guidance or whatever you need.

You might ask how you can blossom when you're going through struggles and my response is that you can if you have your mindset geared toward positive thoughts and keep thinking on happy thoughts. When we think of blossoming, we think of flowers and how in the spring they start blossoming into beautiful flowers after a cold winter. Do you think that they don't have struggles, well they do because if the weather gets too warm and then gets cold again as it often times does in early spring, then those tulips might raise their heads out of the ground too early and the struggles they will be faced with is the fierce weather and somehow they maintain long enough until the spring weather settles down and is warm again and you will see beautiful tulips waving in the wind with the sun shining on them. They have survived the chilly spring temps and now they are a beautiful flower just like when we get through a struggle in our life, and we look back on it and realize that through the struggle we have grown, and we have gotten stronger. Just when we thought we weren't going to be able to make it, God helped us and showed us that He will help us, and He did, and we made it. Don't doubt yourself when going through something because whatever struggle you're facing, think of it like you're climbing a mountain. When we're in the valley we want to be on the mountain top because that's where everything seems to be at peace. When we're in the valley and going through things most of the time it will be a struggle as we're climbing the mountain and trying to get to the top. When we finally do get to the mountain top oh what joy and peace, we feel just knowing that God helped us and didn't forget about us no matter how long we were struggling. Believe me I know the feeling because I was in the valley for about 2 years a few years ago and the struggle was real because I was wondering what was going to happen next. One thing I knew for sure is that God was there with me during my struggles, and I know I came out being a better person and I grew and learned a lot about myself and my Lord and Savior. There might be learning curves when we start a new job; however, there's also learning curves in life because no matter what we face, it's never the same for each person. Life is full of learning curves and it's all about learning and re-learning ourselves and how we act or react to certain things and certain situations and even certain people. I'm sure we all have people in our lives that love to pull on our heartstrings about something. It may be us letting them get us aggravated but somehow, they always know just how to get us stirred up and it seems that we know when we see them that they will stir up some trouble. To blossom, we will need to learn why they always stir up trouble and then act accordingly. Are they doing it just to get us stirred up and if so, maybe we need to ask God to help us not to get stirred up and see if they stop with the trouble they keep starting. It seems that they know what words to use, and they know what our weak points are and use that against us. Let them see that they're not bothering you anymore no matter what words they say to try and get you stirred up because your Crown is staying on straight in your heart because God is helping you to become a better and stronger person. If we strive to become a better person day by day and be the kind of person God wants us to be, then and only then can we blossom when we face challenges in our life. Let God lead and guide you in all the struggles you will face in this life and people will see a change in you and your testimony will be a brighter light for others to see. Let others see your Crown in your heart and let them see that you're a Child of the King and your faith and trust is totally in Him.

We might not like the challenges that come our way; however, it is the challenges that transform us into the person we become.

Have you ever noticed that after you have gone through a challenge you see yourself in a different light and a light of growth and inner strength knowing that you got through another challenge with God's help. There are different kinds of challenges for each person and God is always ready to guide us through each one. God will turn our challenges into opportunities for spiritual growth, personal growth, and development so look at each challenge you face as a steppingstone toward becoming a better you. God will give you guidance to face each challenge with perseverance and wisdom. When you're faced with adversity, just remember who is in control and it's not us it's God and He will anchor us and not let us fall and will give us the assurance that He will accompany us each step of the way. Each trial and challenge that we go through in our journey of life shows us even more how much God loves us, His creation. He promises to never leave you, nor forsake you and He always keeps His promise. As we learn to blossom through each challenge, we're also finding a deeper love for our Creator. The closer you get to God, the more you will realize how much He cares for you and I and how He wants us to be at peace and happy in our journey of life as we go through challenges.

During life's storms and challenges, faith should become an anchor to us that we can grab and hold on to as we tackle whatever is going on in our life. With faith we can transform our spiritual well being into something even greater and better and become more like Jesus. I know we all go along with our life and sometimes don't think much about our spiritual well-being; however, it's just as important as our physical well-being. We go to the doctor when we have aches and pains and are sick so why should we be any different with our spiritual health. God is the great physician, and He can heal us of our sicknesses as well as heal us of any spiritual needs we might have. To tackle challenges in our life and blossom while we tackle them, we need to have our spiritual well-being checkup. We will then be renewed with strength, grace, and hope as we face challenges. As long as we trust God and His plans for our life, we can weather any storm and discover how gracious and merciful God is to us.

Blossoming through our struggles is a lot like a flower blossoming because life's challenges are the fertile soil where our inner strength and hope will take root and grow. We will be growing self-discovery and learned lessons during the adversity of struggles. We talked earlier how adversities are just opportunities for personal and spiritual growth and so we need to embrace the difficulties and hold on and see what God will do and see the new and transformed person we will become because of struggles and challenges in our lives. If you don't have faith, then you won't see God work or see your life change because of your challenges so first you need to fully believe that God will help you when you call out to Him. As we navigate the challenges that come in our life, our inner growth and strength will begin to show, and others will see how you have a story of triumph over difficulties. The Crown we have in our heart shows others our royalty with the King of all Kings, the Lord Jesus Christ. When we are triumphing over our challenges and difficulties in life then our Heart Light is truly showing others our testimony of faith and believing that with God all things are possible. Struggles is what shapes our lives and forms our character into what God wants us to be and carving our spaces for wisdom and strength to take root. As we persist through each storm in our life, the beauty of us blossoming as a flower becomes more evident as our testimony shows the spirit that lives within us to help us to conquer adversities. That spirit is what brings a smile to our face even though we're going through challenges, and we know that our Crown in our heart is sitting up straight for others to see. It's as if others are seeing the Crown of royalty on our head even though it's in our heart because what's in our heart will surface for others to see. What is on the inside will always show on the outside so be mindful of how your Crown is sitting in your heart. Always strive to have the right attitude and always show kindness no matter what situation you're in.

During life's turbulent storms, our growth because of the storm is like a flower bending but not breaking in the fierce wind like the tulips we had talked about before. Look at each challenge as a nourishing rain for the soul allowing us to bloom into the fulness of our potential. I'm sure you've heard people say before that a person might not be showing their full potential, meaning that they could be doing more. The same thing is true with the challenges that we face each day because we can triumph over them, or we can let them knock us down and it's how we look at things as to how we will face challenges. To be able to blossom through our struggles, we need to find strength and resilience in the face of adversity. We need to be able to bounce back even when we're going through struggles. So let's keep that smile on our face and trust God to carry us through and give us strength that we need in order to conquer the challenges we face. Every setback we face will even become a step forward as our personal growth unfolds. Blossoming through struggles is a process and with each new struggle we're able to rise above it with new strength and triumph and we will be able to flourish against all odds. Like a flower seed pushing through the soil, we keep pushing on with each new adversity and break through with renewed strength. Each challenge will become a chapter creating a story in our life where strength, growth and perseverance are blossoming. Our journey of life as we're facing challenges involves putting away any doubts and fears and transforming like a caterpillar into something beautiful. Blossoming through struggles is where we weave threads of courage and tenacity, and our journey will unfold with every challenge giving us strength and wisdom and show others how the adversity has shaped our lives as we overcame the difficulties in our lives. Each struggle we face is like a brick in the construction of our strength, and as we navigate the adversity at the moment, the structure of our character will emerge as we triumph over the adversity. Blossoming through struggles you will create a resiliency that will be able to withstand the storms of your life. Adversity isn't something we endure, it's something we survive, and it creates transforming hues of growth. In adversity we find that blossoms emerge from the fertile soil of our struggles and will create a transformation of resilience of strength and see that with God's help you overcame the difficulties. The journey of blossoming through struggles is in essence an exploration of yourself where each twist and turn in each challenge will give you renewed confidence, strength, and resilience. Each trial that you face will become a landmark in your life guiding you toward personal and spiritual growth. It's not about escaping challenges and struggles but conquering them and turning obstacles into stepping-stones of opportunities toward self-realization into becoming a better you. I hope you're seeing the process and how each struggle that you face is determined by how you are transformed into the renewing of your mind and soul, and you will become a better person after triumphing over your struggles. As you tackle life's challenges, it's a spiritual journey where God's presence will become your guiding light. Through prayer and trust in God, you will see how God's plans unfold for your life and you will see how your challenges and struggles are meant to grow you and transform you into a better person. The roots of your faith need to intertwine with your difficulties where God's wisdom will become the nourishment you need to give you courage and endurance to conquer and triumph over the adversities you face on your journey of life. Your testimony will then be one of the powers of faith guided by God's unwavering presence and helping you to triumph and conquer the adversities you're facing.

I noticed in my own life that how you react to situations is how and to what point you will blossom when you're faced with challenges. So, let's try and make it a point to always strive to do our best whether we're acting or reacting to some situation in our life. It could be something as simple as you took the words of a friend the wrong way and lashed out at them. When we speak words, we need to make sure what we're saying is in the proper tone and the proper words. Some people can say the same words and it will come off differently to some people and some it will bother and some it will not. For example, if there's someone that has lost their dog and you talk about the dog down the street and you might not even be critical of the dog; however, that person will take it that way simply because they lost their dog. We don't always know what's going on in the other person's life so if you have someone lash out at you, take it in stride and try not to lash back. Believe me I've done it because there have been times that a friend was going through something that I wasn't aware of and lashed out at me joking about something, so I just lashed back and say what is your problem. Well, I had to ask God to forgive me first for not acting right and then I had to ask my friend to forgive me. Just like you're wearing your Crown in your heart that will sometimes almost get knocked down, some people might wear their hurts on their shoulder just waiting for someone to knock them off so they can lash out. Remember our Crown is in our Heart and not on our Heads and can never be knocked off because the Crown in our Heart comes from Jesus and the Holy Spirit being in our heart and guiding us each day. Yes, we do make mistakes and I've made plenty in my lifetime and every time we do, we have the Holy Spirit speaking to us telling us that what we said or did wasn't the proper way to act or speak and it has our Crown leaning and God will instruct us how to get our Crown back in the center of our heart. If we keep our Crown where it needs to be, it is then that others can see the peace and joy in our lives and our testimony will be a shining example of God's love. Remember to always watch what words you say and how you say them and let's keep our testimony shining with our Crown standing up straight and strong in our hearts. You never know who is watching you and watching how you act toward certain situations and so we always want others in our path to see God's love in our actions as we journey through this life.

Chapter 3

EMBRACING INNER STRENGTH

We've talked a bit about getting inner strength so now we're going to see how we get inner strength. So how do you get inner strength when you really need it? Do you have certain things that you do to obtain inner strength, or does it come naturally? The best way to get inner strength is to ask God. So, what is inner strength and why do we need it?

Webster's defines strength as "the quality or state of being strong: capacity for exertion or endurance, one regarded as embodying or affording force or firmness." So, if strength is the capacity for enduring some obstacle, what is inner strength? Inner strength is the ability to cope with situations in our life. I'm sure you have heard the word resilience being referred to certain people, well resilience is the same thing as having inner strength. When things are happening in your life that are stressful or emotional and you find the strength somehow to tackle whatever the situation is, then that's inner strength. I'm sure we've all heard stories of people who had to lift heavy objects off their loved one and later told how they didn't know how they did it. It was inner strength within them, and it comes from God. I look at it as a force to be reckoned with that is inside each of us that only comes from God. We are God's creation and He created us in such a way, and He knows what we will need to face in life and so He instilled inner strength in us that we will be able to use in certain situations that will require it. God has equipped us all with what we will face while we're on this earth in our journey of life and when we're faced with challenges that we don't have any humanly idea how to tackle, we have that inner strength that will emerge that we are able to use.

Inner strength isn't needed just for circumstances where we need to lift heavy objects as I mentioned before, it is also needed in our daily lives. As we go on our journey of life, we will be faced with a lot of situations and challenges that will try and trip us up and we need inner strength just to tackle them. It might be as simple as forgiving someone for doing us wrong or having to be patient regarding some issue in your life. Inner strength will teach us to respond calmly instead of reacting impulsively with anger or resentment. Inner strength can also give us self-confidence and determination as well as tolerance. Have you ever needed to be confident about something you're doing, or have you ever needed determination to get a job done, well inner strength will help you with all of that. It's not necessarily the big challenges in our life that drag us down, it is a lot of the little issues in life like keeping your motivation up to redo your garage or paint your kitchen. You may feel a lack of confidence if you're going to speak to a group of people and then after you start speaking you feel confidence in your words. I know the feeling about speaking because I've never been one to speak or sing solos at church without getting extremely nervous and now, I'm speaking on podcasts like I own the stage and it's all because of inner strength. There might also be a situation where you need tolerance to deal with someone and their actions. There are a number of situations where inner strength will help you. With inner strength, you will find that you're more able to forgive others and inner strength will show you that you're in control of your own happiness and it's not dependent on other people and the way they act.

We all have inner strength within us; however, some people have more than others and you might wonder why that is because God gave us inner strength when He created us, and we just need to use the strength inside of us. We need to develop this inner strength if we want to use it correctly. To develop the inner strength we already have, we need to get the proper mindset and we need to look within ourselves and examine ourselves. You will be able to strengthen yourself and become the best version of yourself. You will become better than you thought possible. When you develop your inner strength, you become more trustworthy in the face of any challenge, and you develop a sense of meaning and purpose that can keep you motivated. Developing the inner strength within you is an ongoing process and God will help you to become the better person within you and one with strength and courage. People will see you as a trustworthy and courageous person the more you use your inner strength. Inner strength is necessary in our daily lives in relation to tasks, chores, and even the decisions we make, and it also helps us to meet our goals because it gives us determination to get the job done. Believe me when I tell you it takes inner strength to stay determined to write each chapter in my books I write. With inner strength, you will have the willpower and self-discipline you need. Think of it being like the energizer bunny with the energizer battery that never goes out because inner strength will give you the endurance to carry on in any situation. It will drive you toward any accomplishment you're trying to achieve. What is it that you need to start or finish? Tap into your inner strength to either start something you've been putting off or to finish something you've started yet never finished. Inner strength in essence is assertiveness, courage, and the ability to withstand difficulties and obstacles that come in our lives.

I hope you see why we need inner strength and see that using inner strength in our lives has a lot of benefits. One positive thing is that it enables you to control unnecessary impulses and behaviors. It will also help you with self-esteem and self-control whenever you are faced with difficulties. By using and developing your inner strength you will also be able to have more control over your life. Have you ever noticed people that will fly off the handle at any situation and you think wow they are really out of control and then you see someone that stays calm and is patient throughout a situation and you might think now they have their life all together, well it's how and when you use inner strength as to how well your life stays in control. With God's help in using our inner strength we can learn how to always stay calm and stay in control of any challenge and difficulty in our lives. Inner strength is the ability to keep going even when things are not going the way you think they should go. It's all about taking on life's challenges and taking one step at a time and accepting the challenges and the changes that must be made and keep going. Psalms 73:26 says, "my flesh and my heart may fail, but God is the strength of my heart and my portion forever."

So, you might be asking how you get inner strength because you need it as you might be facing challenges and difficulties in your life. You can get your inner strength by looking inside because your inner strength comes from within yourself. It's the capacity to access a situation, observing our own thoughts and emotions, and the ability to respond wisely and being compassionate. Inner strength is a set of talents and skills given to us by God that helps us survive and thrive in our daily lives. It's a mindset that we all have that drives us to pursue growth in our lives. To find your inner strength, you will need to look inside yourself and see what your aspirations and goals are and what you want to do to better yourself. I'm not talking about making more money or becoming a millionaire even though that would be a great success. I'm talking more about becoming more confident in yourself and your actions and being patient with others and being more determined to achieve the goals we have set that we want done. Here are five ways to help you obtain your inner strength.

1. Practice Self Awareness – discover your aspirations, weaknesses, and strengths. Think about what you like to do in your spare time. What things do you really enjoy?

2. Discover Your Talents – God has given us all talents so look inside and see what your true talents might be.

3. Invest in Your Skills – skills are abilities that you do well and above average. Explore your skills and find ways to improve them. This can be personal and professional skills.

4. Open Yourself to New Experiences – try something new, something you've never done or even thought about doing. This will build creativity, a crucial aspect of inner strength.

5. Be Patient and Positive - if you're not already a positive and patient person, this will be a new learning curve and it's one of the most important in gaining inner strength.

Take advantage of any learning opportunity that life will throw your way. Finding and building your inner strength is probably the smartest thing you can do for yourself. In the past few years, my inner strength has brought me a lot of new opportunities and writing books is one of them. I also found my voice and with that I mean I feel confident when I talk to people now and before I didn't. Looking within yourself and finding what your true talents are and being able to be a better you is what inner strength is all about. People will also notice when they see that you're more confident and calmer in life situations. With inner strength showing your confidence, people will be able to see the Crown in your heart and how your heart is glowing with the love of Jesus. Whether you realize it or not, you have the power within you to overcome any difficulty that life throws at you and the courage to pursue your aspirations and all you must do is look within yourself to find your inner strength. It's a journey of self-discovery and fulfillment as your inner strength goes with you on your journey of life.

Cultivating inner strength is much like cultivating a garden in that we need to water and fertilize and cut out the weeds in our garden to improve the growth and beauty. Cultivating inner strength is accepting our imperfections because we're not perfect and learning from our experiences. While cultivating your inner strength, you're nourishing your mind, body, and spirit because they're all connected, and one affects the other. In the mind, you need to embrace a positive mindset as you see challenges as opportunities for growth. In whatever we face in our lives, there is always some way that we will grow through the challenge and become a better person in the end. In the body, you need to take care of your physical needs through self-care as we've talked about earlier. In the spirit, it involves connecting with your inner self and getting a sense of peace that involves finding purpose in your life. Any challenges that we face need to be faced with a clear understanding and being able to focus on the difficulty at hand and you can do this with inner strength. Through your mindset you can cultivate mental strength as you learn from setbacks that might come and adapt to any changes that may take place. Our body needs to be maintained with good physical health while we see the connections between the mind and body. Through your spirit you can connect to God who created your body and find a sense of purpose for your journey for a more meaningful life. With all three connected the mind, body, and spirit create a balance for your inner strength to help you in whatever challenge that comes your way.

Embracing inner strength is essentially a journey of self-discovery and it includes finding your self-worth, learning from challenges, and finding courage to improve on your imperfections. Inner strength isn't just about overcoming difficulties and challenges that come your way, it's about creating a positive mindset and trusting your capabilities as well as seeing the power that you have within. Inner strength will give you the determination you need to face challenges or get a task completed. It's all about accepting yourself for who you are and learning from mistakes without giving yourself self judgement and appreciating the journey that your life has taken. Do you ever wonder why the life you have went through has been difficult at times and maybe not that easy, well just like a job, it's all about learning curves; however, with our journey of life, we learn from our mistakes, and we grow into a better person with all our experiences. We might see others and think their life seems so easy and they don't go through the same hardships; however, have you thought that they might be going through hardships that you don't see because their inner strength might be stronger. They might have found the power from within and are using it in times of challenges yet to you it seems they have an easy life. Friend, life can be as easy or hard as you make it and if your inner strength is strong, it will make your life seem easier as challenges and situations happen in your journey of life. For a strong inner strength, you will need to set boundaries, prioritize self-care, and develop your mindset to focus on challenges as opportunities for growth. We all fall short sometimes when it comes to self-care because we just don't take the time to access our body and mind the way we should and if we prioritize our self-care, it will help our inner spirit immensely.

It's all about seeing what is within and pulling our strength from the core of our being and that being God who created us. It doesn't matter what situation you're in, if you ask God to help you, He will be there. God will help you with self-care of our body, mind, and spirit because He created them all to be interconnected when he created you. So, by embracing inner strength, you have a powerful alliance with your true self which helps you to navigate life's twists and turns with self-assurance and confidence. Sometimes people want to do things their own way and tackle what life throws at them by being spontaneous and impulsive at each challenge they face, and they never face challenges the same and it's always difficult. By embracing the inner strength that God gave us, we can tackle these challenges with more ease each time a challenge arises. If you haven't looked into the depths of your soul, then maybe it's time to do just that. It involves looking at the shadows and light within and forming a deep connection with your values and allowing self-compassion to guide you on your journey. If we don't have self-compassion, how can we have compassion for others and if we don't have compassion for others, we can be seen as someone who isn't very loving. We need to embrace change with an open heart and open arms accepting what changes need to be made and learning from life and its experiences and understanding that inner strength is not just in triumphs but also in vulnerability. It's ok to be vulnerable sometimes and it's not always a sign of weakness as some might see it. With inner strength, you will cultivate a sense of self-love learning to love yourself and sometimes that's hard to do. You will learn to accept yourself for who you are and unlock the power within you to face life with unwavering strength.

Chapter 4

ELEGANCE IN EVERYDAY CHOICES

We are faced with choices every day no matter what we're doing. Choices may include what we will eat, what groceries we need to buy, and how much money you will have left over after you get paid are just a few choices that everyone will make. Whether the choices we make are right or wrong is dependent on the individual person; however, some choices we make are the same for everyone and still some people will make the wrong choices. Deciding if you will accept Jesus into your heart is a BIG CHOICE and you can make the wrong choice on that if you're not careful. The only correct choice would be to say Yes to accept Jesu because if you choose not to accept Him, then it will affect where you will spend eternity when you leave this earth. Our life here on earth and eternity are all about the choices we make so make your choices wisely. We will talk about the choices we make in our everyday life and how that affects us on our journey in this life. With each choice we make there is also a consequence to that choice. Have you ever thought about the choices you make and how consequences were affected by your choices?

How would you define choices and how are choices and consequences connected? Webster defines choices as "the art of choosing; a number and variety to choose among; care in selecting." Webster defines consequences as "something produced by a cause or necessarily following from a set of conditions." So, we see that even Webster says that whatever choice we make in our journey of life, there will be a consequence to that choice. Every action will have a consequence to follow as a result. Let's be mindful of what choices we make when we're going through difficulties and challenges in our lives because we might not like the consequences that follow our choices. In everything we do in this life we will be faced with struggles and challenges of all kinds that are both good and bad and the choices we make will either give us good or bad consequences. An example would be a married couple that one of the spouses spent their whole paycheck gambling over the weekend and lost all their money and then there isn't any money to buy food or pay bills. The consequence of this person's choice turned out bad and I would hate to be in that person's shoes having to face the other spouse and tell them there isn't any money until next payday. That situation could have gone the other way too because if they had won, they would have extra money on top of their paycheck so before we make any choices no matter how little or big, think about what the consequences might be. The best thing to do in any situation is to pray to God and ask for wisdom in making the correct decision because only God can see the future and only God will know what consequence will come from the choices we decide to make.

When we're making choices in dealing with challenges we face every day, we need to do it with elegance, and you may ask what elegance is and how can I do that when tackling challenges that sometimes are very stressful? Elegance according to Webster is "scientific precision, neatness, and simplicity; refined grace or dignified propriety; dignified gracefulness or restrained beauty in style." We talked earlier about grace and being graceful and with elegance you are being a little more restrained in how we handle challenges in our lives. How are we supposed to be elegant and more restrained as we tackle challenges because I know some challenges wear on you until you get through them. So, let's talk about what it means to tackle our challenges with elegance. When challenges come your way and you become unglued and have an attitude toward someone that's involved in the situation, well that's not showing elegance during difficulties and challenges. To be elegant when we're going through difficulties in our life, it's portraying such an awe-inspiring moment that others take notice. They might know that you're going through something difficult and yet they see you staying calm and being refined the whole time. Just like we talked about your testimony and how people are always watching you, well people also notice how you handle situations and difficulties that arise in your life. When I was having to take radiation treatments, I always had a smile on my face and people noticed because some of the people there would ask me why I always smiled when I came there and to that I would always respond because I have Jesus. People were watching me more than I realized I'm sure and so I'm glad my normal personality was to be smiling. Even through tough situations like I was going through, you can find a reason to smile and be happy and that's what elegance in struggles is all about.

Whatever choices you make on your journey of life, you will be dealing with others in every aspect of your life no matter if it's your normal everyday situations or challenges and difficulties that seem to pop up at the wrong time. Life can be very challenging at times. No matter what you're faced with, think about the words you say and how you say them and their impact on others. You want to always show kindness with your actions and reactions and always show gratitude and be appreciative for the little joys in life as well as the big things. Learn to be a good listener as you connect with others and show a caring attitude. Love others like Jesus loved others. So, elegance means simplicity and thoughtful decisions and being able to focus on quality rather than quantity. It's not the number of people you can help but that one person you did help, and they truly showed their appreciation. By expressing simplicity you're able to turn the ordinary into something refined and graceful. You might get aggravated because your wife always makes you late no matter where you're going and so if you know of a few things you can help her with, then maybe those acts of simplicity will help you to get to your destination quicker. You see it doesn't have to be a huge situation that's going on in our lives, we can change the way we respond to normal everyday situations and use simplicity to make things even better. Elegance blends our mindfulness, compassion, and appreciation with simplicity. Make choices that cause you to reflect on your routine and why you do certain things and allow yourself to be mindful of self-awareness and personal growth.

Even in our normal routines that we do every day, think about why you do them a certain way or why you act a certain way and ask yourself if you changed one small aspect of your routine, would it make life a little easier for you and those around you. Have you ever noticed that when you change the room around that has had the furniture placed a certain direction for years that it gives the room a new feeling. It may even look more breathable, and you might want to stay in that room of your house more often. It's the simplicity of things that make it elegant in how we handle things. It's like giving something new life, a new beginning. It's not a new beginning to start over yet it's a new beginning for growth and maturity and to expand to new horizons. When your heart is heavy with burdens, it's hard to see the simplicity of life and how changes can make a difference. You've heard the saying we've done it that way for years so why change it now. Well, it might be time to change if it's been done that way and never changed. Whatever it is, why not give it new life and give it a breath of fresh air. Let's not be afraid of changes in our lives because sometimes changes are good and bring out the best in us. You've heard people say before that God took them out of their box, well sometimes we get so accustomed to our normal daily routine and don't change that we don't know how it feels to see the possibility of doing something new or even changing one thing to make a difference in our outlook. Think about the things that you love to do or the things that you would love to start doing and take a leap of faith and God will open doors for you to change your direction in this life into doing something new and different. When I started on my journey of writing, I had no idea how my life would change for the better. What if I had not chosen to follow God's direction when He told me that He wanted me to help others by writing books, well I would not have found my voice and I would not have found where my heart is and what touches my heart. Like we said, the choices you make have consequences that can either be good or bad. If the choices you make are to follow God's direction, then you know that will be the right choice and will have a good consequence. Whatever choice you make on your journey of life, always seek God's wisdom and guidance first and know that He will never steer you in the wrong direction and He will help you to make the correct choice.

The main elements of elegance are politeness, respect, and consideration for others. Practicing good manners, using polite and proper language, and showing gratitude is how to create an elegant atmosphere around you and your surroundings. Try being kind to others around you and see what you will get in return. There are plenty of ways to show kindness and caring from holding a door open or opening a door for people at the grocery store. Try holding the umbrella for someone that doesn't have one and numerous other examples of how to be elegant in your everyday choices. One big thing is that we don't need to have an attitude or act like we're better than everyone else because that's not showing elegance. I hope you see that even with little things in our lives or the big things, we make choices every day in one direction or another and we need to show elegance in whatever we do. If our Crown is standing up straight in our hearts, then we won't need to worry if we're showing elegance because our heart is already showing us how to be elegant in our choices and also toward others and in our relationships with others.

I know we all think about how someone dresses when we hear the word elegant and you might not be used to hearing elegance regarding the everyday choices we make; however, it all goes together. You can dress and look elegant and yet be elegant by your actions in your choices and decisions that you make. Those people with true elegance know that it all starts with your thoughts and your mindset. You need to oversee your thoughts as well as your actions. Do you realize that your thoughts will become your reality? If you're thinking that something is bad, then in reality it is bad to you and therefore you will avoid it no matter if it really is something good. It's all about your mindset and what you put into your mind so be careful to always have positive influences that we're putting into our minds. How many times do you watch the mainstream media and through your tv you're infiltrating your mind with all the bad of the world. There might be maybe one or two things on the news that are encouraging but there isn't much of that out there and I don't watch the news at all simply because it's not encouraging and a lot of times depressing. When you put low quality information in your mind, you're setting yourself up for anxiety, frustration, and feeling drained. So, aim yourself with knowledge! Find out and research anything you can because knowledge is power! You can cultivate elegance with a mind full of interesting facts. The biggest challenge for some might be dwelling on things that happened in the past. Let the past stay in the past and look toward the future. Look at your past as lessons learned and move on to what's ahead in the future. If you have the right mindset and are always watching what you put into your mind, then you will have elegance with you in your everyday choices of life.

Elegance comes from within and is a state of mind. Giving a sincere smile to people we meet along our journey and just the ability to put others at ease will embody elegance in our actions. It's about embracing a refined approach to your actions as well as your choices. We need to embrace a poised demeanor and cultivate mindfulness in our actions. Always be watching your posture, movement, and speech because a person's body language will tell a lot about the person even without them saying a word. In stressful situations, we need to maintain calmness and stay composed. Your mindset allows you to be fully present and engaged in the situation at hand and that's why we need to only feed our mind with positive things and not get our mind bogged down with negativity. Besides being unhealthy for our bodies, putting negativity in our mind will make it to where we can't fully concentrate on the tasks at hand and doesn't show elegance in our interactions. Elegance is an individual expression that comes from inner grace, refined taste, and attention to detail. If you want to have elegance in your actions as well as your choices in life, you need to think about your mindset and what is within you and what truly affects your heart. Also help others to see that by elegant living in our interactions and choices in life, we will be able to show more kindness and consideration for others. Remember one small act of kindness or even just a smile can do wonders for someone and help them more than we know.

With elegance in our everyday choices, we can turn mundane moments into graceful and sincere expressions of thoughtful decisions that show simplicity and refinement. Elegance is our conscious choice to infuse ordinary everyday actions with a touch of grace. Simply put, it's the words we choose and the gratitude we share that shows elegance in our everyday choices through simplicity and refinement. We've talked some about grace and how it is similar to elegance and they both have a sense of refinement. Grace on one hand shows a natural and effortless poise and shows through one's demeanor. Elegance on the other hand involves a conscious choice to add refinement to our actions or choices. Grace is more of an inherent quality, while elegance is a deliberate pursuit combining thoughtfulness and style to push the ordinary into something bigger and better. Elegance is the result of thoughtful choices aimed at having a pleasant outcome. Grace and elegance seem to go together, and they offer distinct dimensions to the art of living gracefully. Grace is an internal character trait while elegance is an external manifestation that will transform the ordinary into the extraordinary and together, they will weave a tapestry of refined living for us all. So, in everyday choices on our journey of life, you can't have one without the other.

Chapter 5

POWER OF A POSITIVE PERSPECTIVE

We've already been talking about how negativity isn't good for your mind and now we're going to talk about how staying positive and having a positive outlook can help you and enrich your mindset more than you might realize. So, what does it mean to be positive and how can you have power in being positive? All my life I've tried to maintain a positive outlook in everything and most of the time I was a very positive and a chirpy happy person; however, there are times when things happen in life, and we must keep talking to ourselves and keep praying to God because you need a reason to stay positive and keep smiling. Those of you who read my last book remember that there was a 2-year span that I was going through a lot of things in my life and so it was hard for me to stay positive. I maintained and did stay positive, and it was only with God's help. I was wondering what was going to happen next with everything that was happening from cancer, to job loss and several other things and then God showed me that staying positive was the only way to have power over my difficulties. So, we're going to see how you can have power through having a positive perspective in every difficulty on your journey of life.

First let's see what it means to be positive and then we will look at how we can have power through being positive in every situation we face on our journey in this life. Positive simply means to be hopeful and confident and thinking only of the good rather than the bad. I'm sure we've all been around people that are negative, and they see the bad in everything and even when the sun is shining, they will find something bad to say about that. So, to have a positive perspective on everything, your heart must be filled with positivity and get rid of any negativity. To keep your Crown straight and not having to straighten it all the time, keep a positive outlook on life. No matter what is going on, there's always something positive to find in every situation and challenge we will face. Being positive and staying positive will also enrich our lives and keep us happier and when we're happier, we are able to show our love and care to others more easily. Positive in a simplistic state means to think in an optimistic way and to always expect the best outcomes and good results and a worry-free state of mind and one that always looks on the bright side. There are several ways to stay positive.

1. Enjoying your present moment – no matter what you're going through enjoy it to the best of your ability.

2. Do not worry about the future – only God knows what the future holds, so there's no reason to be worrying about it anyway. Just put it in God's hands and let Him take care of it and have more peace in your life by not worrying.

3. Focus on the present and not the past – whatever you're doing, focus on what you're trying to do and don't focus on the past and what has happened because you want to concentrate on successes and not failures. Concentrate on what needs to be done now and

thinking in the present and not the past will give you a clearer mindset on how to get it done. It could be a project you're working on, or it could be a situation you're having to deal with.

4. Stay happy and good natured – keep a smile on your face no matter what you're having to deal with and keep a good-natured spirit within you. Don't take things people might say personally because that will damper your positive spirit.

By being positive and staying positive, you will be using a lot of emotions that you might not be used to if you're not already a positive person. There will be emotions of joy, love, and inspiration and positive minded people choose to have constructive and good feelings and emotions rather than negative and unhappy feelings. Positivity brings thoughts of courage, self-esteem, and success. Think with words of I can, and this is possible. My favorite words are Yes and take a step. If you say No you're staying in the same place and if you say Yes and take a step forward, you're moving toward a new direction and being positive and staying positive will get you there with God's help. You can stay positive even in bad situations because I stayed positive in a lot of situations I went through in my lifetime. You will just learn from the situations, you will grow and mature because of them, and use the knowledge you learned while going through situations to improve with anything you're faced with in the future. It's vital to monitor what influences your mind and your life because if you get too many negative views, it can try to influence the positivity in your life. We all know that the news nowadays isn't always pleasant and most of it is negative, so don't let it seep into your subconscious mind or it will try and rule your life. If you keep filling your mind with positive thoughts and emotions, then the negative influences will not have a chance to try and overrule your mind. That's what I'm talking about when I say you have power in positive perspective because we are going to be influenced by the negativity in this world; however, it's how we handle it that will affect our mind. If we don't let it affect us and keep staying positive, then that's when we have power to keep our mindset staying positive no matter what we face on our journey.

You might think that you're already a positive person and that negative influences won't bother you, yet they will, and I know because I've always been a positive person and I had negative influences to try and overtake my positive outlook. We need to always be on guard to safeguard our mind. We will always watch out for our children and don't want them hanging around people with bad influences so we need to do the same thing with ourselves and our mind because some things it might be hard trying to release from your mind. Fill each day with a little optimism, happy thoughts, and do something useful to improve your life and the lives of others around you. This will help you to continue to grow into a powerfully positive person who can tackle any situation in their life with positivity and not negativity.

Keeping a positive mindset will also reduce stress and we all know that stress is not good for you. Positive thinking is a vital key to effectively managing stress and has many health benefits so let's get the negativity out of our lives and improve our health. The top key health benefits to keeping a positive mindset and reducing stress are:

1. Increased life span
2. Lower levels of distress and pain
3. Greater resistance to illness

4. Better psychological and physical well-being

5. Better coping skills during hardships and times of stress

Having a powerful positive outlook will help you to cope better with stressful situations which will in turn reduce the harmful health effects of stress on your body. When your state of mind is generally more optimistic, you're better able to handle everyday stress in a more constructive way. Let's all work to become more positive and have a more optimistic outlook whether you're mostly negative or like myself have always been positive because as you see it can give you great health benefits. You might be asking about how you stay positive while you're going through negative things that affect your life. Well, we all have challenges and situations that pop up in our lives that aren't that positive and so yes, it's hard sometimes to keep a positive perspective yet it can be done. First you need to call out to God to help you and He will help you to stay more positive than negative in whatever you're facing. I'm sure we've all heard people say oh my whole life has been like that and it's no changing it and that's why I stay so negative and so to that I say, "with God all things are possible and just give God a chance and see what only He can do with your life. Positive thinking is taking a realistic and optimistic view of yourself and your life and others in your life. It doesn't mean ignoring problems or tricking yourself into being happy because that will only be short term if you try to do that. I've seen some people, and they look like they have a fake smile and I wondered if they were trying to make others believe they were happy when they weren't. Having a positive outlook and staying positive in our mindset is on the same rule because you can't pretend to be positive when you're not because it will only last a short time and people will see your true self and your negativity will come out. To have the power of positivity in your life, we all need to have true positivity and that means being positive in everything no matter whether it is a good or bad situation.

Learning how to be more positive is possible no matter if you're a negative person or a slightly positive person. We need to learn how to think more optimistically, change our habits and lifestyle, and move toward our goals. Your words are more powerful than you realize and if we think more closely about how we say things it might change your life. How many times have we said oh I don't feel good I think I'm getting sick yet what would have happened if we changed our words and said I feel fine and I don't have a worry in the world. Don't speak negativity into the world always claim the positive and speak positivity into the world. Yes, sometimes we don't feel good and sometimes we do get sick; however, is it because we already spoke it into the world with our words. Sometimes my work might be slow, and I will say that I wish it was busier and then we get slammed so was it because I spoke it into the world well my supervisor sure thinks so. All I'm saying is watch your words and try to always say positive words no matter who you're talking to or what the situation might be. Focus on the good things about you and your life and you can start being a more positive person. You might say well I don't have anything good to say about myself well you do because you're a Child of God and He created You. Don't compare yourself to other people because we are all different and all have individual personalities and traits. Whatever flaws you might have, realize that we all have flaws and unless you tell someone about your flaws most people don't notice your flaws. Forgive yourself for past mistakes and ask yourself what you can learn from your mistakes. Learning to forgive yourself is a big factor in being positive because some people find it very hard to forgive themselves and even to love themselves. It will be hard to stay positive if you can't love yourself and forgive yourself for past mistakes. If this is you, please go look in the mirror and say to yourself I am lovable, and God loves me, and my mistakes are in the past and I'm going to move to the future and see how God can help me to improve. Talking to yourself in a kind and encouraging way can help you to love yourself and then love others better and in turn will improve your mood and help you to stay positive with an optimistic outlook on life. Mindfulness, also known as being present in the moment, can improve your mood and wellbeing and you will start to experience fewer negative thoughts and emotions. Take 7 seconds and do deep breathing and be thankful for everything you see around you. Focus on the good things in life and look for things that make life more enjoyable. Spend time with people that make you feel good because their happy upbeat mood will rub off on you and you will be a happy upbeat person. Working toward your goals can also make you feel more positive about yourself. You might say that you don't have any goals, well everyone has goals and aspirations and things they have been wanting to do so think about the things that you love to do to help you see what goals you have.

Having a positive perspective gives us the power to turn challenges into opportunities and learning experiences and inspiring actions. It can influence how we navigate our journey of life with optimism and hope leading to personal growth and fulfillment in our lives. It can be a mental framework where people can interpret situations in a constructive light if we focus on solutions rather than problems. Having a positive mindset will help you in any adversity by viewing setbacks as learning experiences and by cultivating gratitude, you can bounce back from adversities with greater strength. A positive mindset will also help to have better interpersonal relationships and you will see the potential for growth and improvement in yourself and others. The power of positive thinking could influence the behavior and decision making of people leading them to make choices that contribute to their overall well-being. It's not about denying the existence of challenges but approaching them with a mindset that will seek opportunities for growth and positive change, and it will shape your attitudes and actions and life experiences. Having a positive perspective in your life will also get others looking at you and seeing how your life has changed for the better especially if you were a negative person before and now, you're more confident and have a positive outlook on life even through any difficulties in your life. Remember there is always someone watching you and so we need to always have the right testimony and that includes acting positively in life.

Cultivating a positive perspective can always impact our lives in so many ways. It can improve our mental well-being by focusing on the good in every situation as well as giving us enhanced problem-solving skills and strengthening our relationships with others. Maintaining a positive outlook can be crucial in our lives because it helps us to navigate life's ups and downs with optimism and resilience. Whatever situation we're faced with we train our brains to either be positive or negative in how we react to the situation. By being positive and focusing on the good in every situation, we train our mindset to see possibilities rather than limitations. It can also improve problem solving skills because we are not stuck in a negative mindset and positivity encourages creativity and new avenues for finding solutions.

By being positive rather than negative, we look for the silver lining in every situation we're faced with. By seeing the silver lining in every situation, we will always see possibilities instead of obstacles and this allows us to approach difficulties in our lives calmly and clearly and stress free. It shows us that any setbacks are only temporary and that every experience shows us something valuable to learn. If we adopt a positive outlook, it will enhance our problem-solving skills when we're faced with challenging situations. We will maintain an optimistic mindset rather than becoming discouraged or overwhelmed and so we will approach any difficulty with clarity and creativity. By staying positive, we can find opportunities that might not have been there before because we are staying open minded and looking for a silver lining even in adversity. Unexpected opportunities that arise will give us growth and innovation to allow us to navigate difficulties with resilience and hope. So, let's get a positive outlook if we don't have one and if we do have one, let's keep getting better at showing our positive perspective to those around us.

Chapter 6

SERENITY IN THE STORM

We all go through storms in our lives that range from small storms to huge storms, and we might wonder how we will get through the storms in our lives. I've had a lot of storms in my life over the years and some I did wonder how I was going to make it, But God took over and then the storm was calm seas. So how can we have serenity in the storm? How is it even possible that we can stay calm while we're going through storms in our lives? First let's see what serenity is and then we will talk about how we can have serenity while we're going through storms. Webster defines serenity as "a state of freedom from storm or disturbance; peacefulness." Serenity also means the absence of mental stress or anxiety. It's in essence a state of being calm, peaceful, and untroubled. If you are feeling serenity with life's ups and downs, it means you're not bothered by any challenges that come your way. You handle them with ease and then go on about your life. It is the ability to find inner peace and tranquility even though you're going through storms in your life. You have a mindset and an emotional state that is calm and centered even in the middle of storms. We talked about mindsets earlier and inner strength and now we see that serenity is also connected to your mindset and your inner strength. If you have the inner strength to deal with the storm, then you will have the inner peace you need and the mindset to tackle it with peace and calmness. The key element in serenity is mindfulness and you will be fully present in the moment and focus on the moment at hand and have clarity and composure as you handle the storm in your life. By accepting the current circumstances, you can also direct your energy toward what you can control because some things in our life we can't control. Even with storms that come into your life with things you can't control, you can still have serenity through the storm because you can still be focused on the current situation. Serenity in the storms of our lives is about navigating life's ups and downs with grace and inner calmness, which is all about our mindset and how we perceive things. It will give us a foundation for emotional well-being even when we're faced with storms. People will serenity in the storms of life will emerge from their storm with a sense of inner peace and strength. Like we talked about before, it's all about your mindset and how you handle storms.

One aspect of serenity is the concept of self-awareness, and we need to understand our own reactions and emotions in the face of challenges. Self-awareness can also lead to greater decision-making and the ability to stay centered and focused even while in a storm. Serenity can be seen as surrender; however, it's not, but rather showing that there's no need to control every aspect of situations that arise. Just accepting that some things are beyond our control can alleviate stress and give us a sense of serenity by focusing on what we can change. Serenity involves self-awareness, gratitude, and willingness to surrender control when necessary. So, we can not only weather the storm but find peace even in the middle of a storm. I've had plenty of storms in my life that I had no control over and so you need to step away in those situations and just be at peace until the storm settles down. When you're going through storms that you have no control over, it's hard to not try and do something to fix the problem; however, sometimes when you try and fix the problem, you might even make it worse. Give it to God and let Him take care of it because it's out of your control and nothing you can do will fix the situation. I'm the type of person who likes to try and fix everything and everyone so I had to learn this lesson and so now when I see things I can't fix, I just step away and stay calm and be at peace and let God take care of it in His way and in His time. We also need to understand and manage all our emotions in a healthy way so rather than being overwhelmed or suppressing our emotions which is what I used to do, we can learn to navigate them in a skillful way to have a more serene emotional state even in the storms of life. Developing a growth mindset where we learn and grow through our storms can impact how you react to adversity. Like we talked about before, seeing challenges as opportunities for learning and personal development can help us to be serene in difficulties. Serenity involves restructuring the way your brain thinks, emotional management, effective communication, and a growth-oriented mindset that will give you a proper understanding on how to not only survive a storm but being able to thrive in the storm with peace and calmness.

We will always have some kind of storms come into our lives while we are living on this earth and how we handle them makes all the difference. People will be watching how you act and react to storms and situations that arise and how you act and react tells a lot about your heart and what's in your heart. What is truly in your heart will come out in your actions, so you better make sure to have a pure heart. If your heart isn't filled with love, then when someone does you wrong others will see your actions as that of someone who needs lessons on loving. We should all have love, gratitude, and forgiveness in our heart and things we shouldn't have in our heart are revenge, hatred, bitterness, and an unforgiving spirit. Galatians 5:22-23 says, "But the fruit of the Spirit is love, joy, peace, longsuffering, gentleness, goodness, faith, meekness, temperance: against such there is no law." I'm sure you have seen people the way they carry themselves and when you see them, you might say they have a true heart, and you might not even know them, but you can tell just by their actions in everyday life. They might smile at everyone they meet and say hello and they act like they don't have a care in the world. It's those kinds of people that the world takes notice of because they are different. The world we live in is made up of people that are fighting because of different things whether it be your race or whether you're male or female and nowadays people aren't even sure about that because they're not happy with how God created them and want to change to another gender. Nowadays it's not really who you are, it seems to be who you want to be identified as and so for me I identify as a Child of the King and I'm happy the way God created me, and I wear His Crown in my Heart. If we want to make a difference in this world, we need to start with ourselves and be happy with ourselves and improve on what we can and treat others with love and respect instead of always having an attitude toward people and situations. Just because you don't like a person, or a situation doesn't mean you need to have an attitude because you never know what that person might be going through. Like the Bible verse says, "Create in me a clean heart dear Lord," and we can always clean up our heart and be more loving to others. That's what serenity is all about, having a pure heart and being able to not only treat others with respect but also showing others that when you're going through a storm, you can still have peace and joy in your heart. I've heard people say this world has gone crazy and I might have even said it and sometimes I think that it might be going crazy because there aren't enough people willing to take a stand and show others what a true heart really is and how we can truly respect others and their opinions without getting mad about it and always having bad attitudes. The next time a situation arises, or you have a storm come into your life, think about how you respond and how you're showing others your actions and try to show them the actions from a true heart.

How do you get serenity and have a clean heart. First thing is to make sure you have Jesus Christ in your heart and if you do then He will help you to have a clean heart. There are sometimes that you need to go back to Him and ask Him to renew your heart and make it clean again because we get so bogged down with this earth that things get in our heart that don't need to be there. If you don't have Jesus in your heart, then pray to Him and ask Him to come into your heart and repent of all your sins and you can even find a local church to help you find Jesus as well. What I'm saying is there are several ways to find serenity so you can have calmness and peace when going through the storms of life, yet the main way to get serenity is through Jesus Christ our Lord and Savior and He is the one that gives you the Crown to wear in your Heart. Another way to find serenity is by looking at your heart and your life and seeing what you need to change. If you have worry in your mindset and in your heart, it will be hard to have serenity during storms. Worry hurts you more than anyone else because if you worry about something you can't change, you're missing the sunshine of the day where you could be smiling and happy. Worrying is nothing more than being anxious over a difficulty we don't know what will happen tomorrow so why worry about it. We might all get concerned when we're in a storm, just don't let your concern turn to worry and then anxiety. Finding serenity and being able to practice it during storms in our life includes focusing on the present moment and showing gratitude for everything around you. You can even get calm by doing breathing exercises for meditation. Try engaging in things that bring you joy and peace like reading, listening to music or even walking outside. Another way is to get a journal and make note of all the positive aspects of your life and you will find that you can be grateful for a lot of things in your life. Clean out the clutter in your mind just like you do in your closet. We put things in our mind every day that clutter up the good stuff. One good way to find serenity is to let go of things you have no control over. Prioritize self-care and make sure you're getting enough sleep and that you have the proper diet and you're putting the right foods into your body and you're getting exercise. All these things will affect your mental well-being as well as your physical well-being and in turn can affect your mindset. Your mindset needs to be on the right track too if you're trying to find serenity in your life. Surround yourself with positive influences and limit the negative exposures that might come into your life. Journaling is a good outlet I've found for writing down your thoughts and emotions. After you write them down, then let them go and focus on something else. If you have emotional baggage wearing you down, release it through forgiveness for yourself or other people. Practice self-compassion and be kind to yourself like you would other people. Sometimes we're nicer and more forgiving to others than we are to ourselves. Focus on what truly matters and put everything else to the side. If it's not going to matter, why even be concerned over it. An old saying is let tomorrow take care of itself because a lot of times we worry about something that hasn't even happened yet or may not happen and that is stealing our joy for today. You can also volunteer to help people and that will show acts of kindness and give you a sense of purpose and connection. Sometimes we go about our daily lives not really thinking that much about others and wouldn't dare volunteer anywhere yet that's where you will be able to find serenity because when you volunteer, you're helping others and you're showing kindness and respect for others no matter what shape they might be in. When you volunteer to help, it will show you that your life isn't that bad, and you can shine a light for others to help them. You might not realize it, but one small act of kindness can help someone more than we think. Just a smile can go a long way in someone's life that really needs a smile.

Serenity is important in so many ways when you're going through a storm and when others around you are going through a storm. If someone around you is going through a storm, then you can show them calm and peace in their storm rather than being all anxious and concerned about their situation. By showing them peace, they will see how they can get through their storm more easily. Serenity is important for mental well-being as it will give us inner calm and peace and reduces stress. With serenity and having a mental well-being, we can have our brains do clearer thinking and make better decisions. We're also able to focus better and we can cope with challenges that come up and we have an overall better mindset. We want to have serenity to have long lasting benefits on our mental and emotional well-being. There are several benefits of having serenity in our lives such as these.

1. Stress Reduction – serenity is a natural stress reliever by calming our nervous system.
2. Improved Mental Health – lower levels of anxiety and depression giving a more stable mindset.
3. Enhanced Focus and Clarity – when we're free from distractions and have inner peace, we can make better decisions and think more clearly.
4. Increased Resilience – serenity helps us to cope with life's ups and downs and we bounce back quicker from any setbacks.
5. Promotes a Positive Outlook – optimism can affect how we respond to challenges.

I hope you see that if we have serenity in our everyday challenges and storms in our lives, that it affects not only one part of our body, but it affects our whole body. Our mindset, our wellbeing, and emotions are all affected and by having serenity it will give us an overall improved quality of life. We will look at things differently and we will have a clearer head and be able to make more informed decisions on situations that arise in our lives. The one benefit of serenity is how it helps our health because it decreases our stress levels as well as helping our anxiety and depression we might have. The attribute of serenity gives you an emotional balance and a positive mindset toward yourself and others. Serenity comes from within and sometimes we need to look within ourselves to find it, especially if it's clouded over by other things that don't need to be in our mind. So always be aware of what you're putting in your mind and make sure to take a closer look at yourself and what's within to see if you need to do a cleaning to get rid of wrong thinking and other bad attitudes. To be able to have joy and peace and calmness in the storms that come in our lives, we can only do that with serenity in our hearts and minds. We need to be able to look at a situation in our life with resilience and know when we need to step away and other times when we can make informed decisions with a clear mindset. The next time a storm arises in your life, just take a deep breath and be grateful for the storm and take it all in stride and stay calm as you decide what you need to do to make informed decisions with ease and you can do it as long as you have serenity in your mindset. Remember it's all about what's in your mind and how you handle situations that will allow you to either be calm and make informed decisions or to be anxious and be unsure in your decision making. Keep as many positive influences around you as possible and try to keep away from negative influences.

Chapter 7

CROWNED CONFIDENCE

∞∞∞

Confidence is something that I've had to learn because I never was confident in myself in anything I did yet other people would tell me how wonderful I was at doing something. My confidence came when I finally realized who I was, and it wasn't anything that I did or didn't do, it was knowing that I am a Child of The King! Jesus Christ my Lord and Savior created me and knew what I would do in my lifetime, and He knew I would make mistakes and He knew there would be several learning curves. I was influenced by other people and their actions and compared them to myself, and we can't do that and have the confidence that we need. It's not the confidence that oh I'm doing so great but the confidence that you know who you are, and you know where you've come from and you're aiming to make your future great with God's help. Even as an Author with each book I write, sometimes I ask myself, will anyone want to read my books and then God comes back and says you're encouraging and helping people to find Jesus and to see how to get through difficulties in their own lives. We must always do a confidence checkup to see if our confidence is in our own mind and are we doing what we do for man's glory or is there a bigger picture. The answer is Yes that there is a bigger picture, and that picture is one of God and His glory and grace and seeing that it is with Him helping us that we are doing a great job, and He is the one that will give us the confidence that we need. I don't know if you're like me not realizing your confidence or not wanting to admit it, but we all need to be confident in ourselves and what we're doing. Confidence will also help us to do a better job at what we do.

What is the definition of confidence? Why do we really need confidence? What will being confident do for you? Webster defines confidence as, "a feeling or consciousness of one's powers; the quality or state of being certain." So, confidence is essentially faith in oneself and one's powers without showing conceit or arrogance. Confidence is trusting yourself and your ability to succeed. Confident people are usually happy people because they make their own happiness, and they know how hard they have worked to succeed. Being confident is the ability to meet life's challenges and to succeed. It is a realistic sense of one's abilities and trusting yourself and believing in yourself. When I became a best-selling author, that boosted my confidence, and I knew I could write books that people wanted to read. Before I might have had the assurance that I could write good books but when I became best seller and I knew people were buying my books because they were enjoying what I was writing, then I really had confidence in myself, and I began to trust myself that I was doing a good thing and doing what God wanted me to do. Self-confident people don't need others' approval because they have their own approval within themselves, and they know when they've done a good job. Some people have low self-esteem and that is when you lack confidence about who you are and what you can do. People with low self esteem are afraid of making mistakes and letting people down. When I was younger and I was lacking confidence, I'm sure I had low self- esteem because I was always trying to please other people and not pleasing myself and not trusting my own self in what I could do. Everyone isn't born with a sense of confidence and sometimes it becomes hard to develop confidence. I must admit it took me a few years to get my confidence up to where it is now and it's all because God was helping me and showing me things. A confident person will do what they believe is right even when the crowd thinks it's not right and a confident person will take a stand for what they believe. Someone with true self confidence will accept who they are even with their imperfections. You will like yourself and feel good about yourself without being egoistic. When I became the best seller of my last book, I could feel my confidence soaring because I knew I could do it and I did, and I kept telling myself look what I did. Having confidence makes you feel good about yourself.

Crowned Confidence is a strong and self-assured mindset. You will see that your mindset is affected by a lot and what's in your mindset will affect how you deal with life and its challenges and difficulties. The crown that's in your heart needs to have confidence to face life and its challenges. With a crown of confidence, you believe in yourself, your abilities, and you recognize your strengths, and you will set goals for yourself and face challenges with a positive attitude. To have a crown of confidence, you need to acknowledge your achievements both big and small, reflect on your skills, and embrace your uniqueness, and surround yourself with positive influences and focus on personal growth. You will need to practice self-care and maintain a healthy balance in your life and challenge negative thoughts and replace them with positive influences that reinforce your self-esteem. Creating your crown of confidence is ongoing where you celebrate progress and learn from setbacks and continue to work on you and your self-assurance. Your crown of confidence will eventually become a powerful symbol of your inner strength and belief in yourself. Self-assurance and confidence are similar, yet they are different in ways too. Confidence is a belief in one's abilities, appearance, or judgment. It shows a positive outlook and a sense of certainty in various areas of your life. Self-assurance is more specific, and it relates to your inner conviction and belief in your capabilities and shows confidence as understanding one's strengths and trust in your decisions and actions. Confidence is like the top layer and self-assurance is underneath in the second layer. Confidence shows up in professional endeavors or personal challenges while Self assurance is a strong internal foundation that gives us a strong sense of security in our capabilities. Both give us a positive and resilient mindset. Confidence arises from experiences, and achievements and can fluctuate based on external factors. Self-assurance on the other hand is rooted in self-awareness, a deep understanding of one's values, and a belief in one's capabilities and is not shaken by external factors. Confidence can be seen as an outward display of one's certainty while Self assurance can be seen as quiet inner strength, and we need them both. Look at confidence as situation specific and self-assurance as constant aspects of one's life. They go hand in hand, yet they are different from each other in how they both relate to our mindset.

Those with higher self-esteem are generally happier and more satisfied. I can attest to that because when I didn't have the confidence I have now, it didn't seem like I was as happy or satisfied. There is just something about being confident with who you are and what you're doing that gives you a good feeling inside. If you're lacking confidence or want more confidence, there are several ways to build self-confidence.

1. Practice Self-care – take care of yourself by eating good and sleeping well. Find out what your needs are and see what really makes you feel good and happy. Try being grateful for everything in order to reduce any stress.

2. Build Positive relationships – try to only have positive influences in your life and if you do have negative influences, don't let them bring you down. Being around positive people and positive influences can raise your confidence level.

3. Work on a growth mindset – being confident is a learning process and you need to learn to love and trust yourself completely. Grow your mind and don't let it be fixed and not learn new things. Growing your mind can help a lot with confidence.

4. Challenge yourself – find things you want to do and set goals and move forward with a new focus and new confidence with no fear.

5. Practice self-affirmations – being able to tell yourself that you trust yourself and that you trust your abilities in what you're doing. Be proud of yourself! The more you can tell yourself how great you are, the more confidence you will get.

We've talked about what confidence is and how to increase your confidence and how it relates to self-assurance. Now let's talk about what being confident will do for you and how you will handle life better with all its challenges and difficulties. You might say that you're fine without a lot of confidence yet think about how much greater your life will be and how much happier and more grateful you will be. We're not talking about confidence to the point of being arrogant and vain but confidence where you're so self-assured of yourself and your abilities that you feel like you could conquer anything that comes your way. Being confident will give you an extra good feeling within while also showing others around you that you're filled with positivity and not negativity. While others may hold their head down and not want to talk to anyone they meet in their path, those with confidence will smile and greet everyone that comes in their path and they're always happy for another day. When you have confidence, there are a lot of benefits you can have in different areas of your life. Confidence will give you increased performance in your abilities. Whatever you need to do in life, you will be able to do it better with confidence in your stride. I've heard people say that they could never do public speaking or never sing a solo in church yet if you have the confidence that you can do those things, then you will be able to do them. All you need to do is tell yourself that you can get up in front of people and speak and you will do it with ease. I've never spoken on stage or been on tv, yet I am doing podcasts talking to strangers about the books I write and I'm able to do that because I have the confidence to do it. I didn't get the confidence by myself, and it was through God helping me that I have the confidence I need to speak boldly to others about my books. No matter what your job is or what you do on your journey of life, confidence will enhance your effectiveness in whatever you do. Confidence can also increase your communication more effectively and you will be better able to express your thoughts and ideas to others. I was always shy and an introvert and with confidence, God has shown me that I have a voice and I have turned into a people person, and I love to talk to others. You too can achieve any dreams and goals you might have with confidence. Of course, there will be setbacks occasionally because we all have them; however, with confidence you will be able to bounce back quicker. Those that believe in themselves will see challenges as learning opportunities and growth and will keep a positive outlook on whatever life throws their way.

We talked about self esteem earlier and how it's linked to confidence and when you have confidence, it also helps your mental health and well-being because you perceive yourself in a better way than if you didn't have confidence. Also, the way others perceive you will give you greater opportunities like promotions at work and personal growth. For some reason it seems like people are naturally drawn to confident people and maybe it's because they have a special air about them yet whatever the reason, being confident can help you succeed in many ways. Confidence is reflected in your body language whether it be a firm handshake or upright posture, it shows competence and assurance to others. You will also have less anxiety and stress because when you believe in yourself and trust your abilities, you're less likely to feel overwhelmed and you won't worry about feeling like you're failing or feeling uncertain about your capabilities. Confidence will also give you a positive influence toward others. You will be able to inspire others, whether family or friends, to go after their goals and inspirations with confidence. Having confidence will impact all areas of your life from your relationships with others to your career as well as your mental well-being and your emotional needs and will promote mindset growth. It will help you to tackle any challenges that come your way as well as take risks that you might not have taken before, and you will have personal growth and achievement in your journey of life. Better decision making is another benefit of confidence because you will be able to trust yourself and not have doubts and you will make more decisive decisions. You will trust your instincts and know that you made the right decision. You will be able to stand up for yourself and tell others what you need and assert your rights in a better way. Confidence has a lot to do with your mindset as we've been talking about and with confidence you will be more able and willing to take risks and be more creative and explore and see what you can do and to think outside the box. Confidence will also keep you motivated to attain your goals because when you believe in yourself, you will stay on the course and set higher goals and achievements. You will have a sense of satisfaction on your life journey, and you will take pride in your accomplishments and success, and you will have fulfilment and satisfaction in your life. Like we talked about earlier, the big positive benefit of having confidence is not so you can become a confident leader which you will be able to do but the main reason is that it keeps you healthier. Confidence will give you better mental and physical health with lower levels of stress, anxiety, and depression. It may take some time and effort yet the rewards you will receive will be worth the effort it takes.

Overall, confidence will enhance your life in many ways from your relationships to your health, and to the way people respond to you. You will feel more self-assured and more trusting of yourself, and you won't be worried about what people think of you. Confident people approach challenges with a proactive mindset and will find solutions rather than problems. You will also be able to adapt to changes more easily and most people don't like changes, yet with confidence you will be able to adapt easier. You will also be able to set healthy boundaries in your life to promote self-care and well-being. Self-care is important in any aspect whether you have confidence or not because if we don't care for ourselves and our bodies, then other issues will arise. It all seems to go together. Our body works together just like our mindset and emotions and mental health work together. Confidence will cultivate a mindset of gratitude and positivity and you will appreciate your strengths, accomplishments, and blessings you have in your life. You might say that confidence is just an attribute like someone's personality yet it's not because it helps you obtain growth, success, and fulfillment in every aspect of your life. You can overcome difficulties, take advantage of opportunities that come your way and hopefully make a difference in the lives of people around you. So, I hope you see that being confident is not a requirement in this world we live it; however, it makes life a whole lot easier and it helps us to concentrate more on keeping the Crown in our heart on straight and glowing for others to see. 2 Timothy 1:7 says, "For God gave us a spirit not of fear but of power and love and self-control." Psalms 27:3 says, "Though an army encamp against me, my heart shall not fear; though war arise against me, yet I will be confident." Even God's Word says we can be confident and if you're seeking to be more confident, ask God to help and He will help you to become more confident.

Chapter 8
FINDING GRATITUDE

Why is it that some people find it so hard to be grateful for everything they have whether it is their family or job or other blessings in their life? Some people just don't see the need to be grateful for what they have or maybe they don't realize that they could lose everything in an instant. No matter how big your life is, whether you live in a luxury townhome in Beverly Hills, California or whether you live in a mobile home in Alabama, we all have something to be grateful for. To keep your Crown on straight in your heart, we need to learn gratitude. First, let's define what gratitude really is and then we will see why we should be grateful. Webster defines gratitude as, "appreciative of benefits received; pleasure or contentment." So, when you're grateful you're not only thankful for what you have received but you're also appreciative. Nowadays it's hard to find people that truly appreciate a gift being given to them. This new generation doesn't seem to understand the idea of being appreciative and grateful. When I was growing up, we were raised to not only be thankful for everything but to also be appreciative of things that we receive whether we like the things received or not. Sometimes it's good just to think about our life and everything we have in our life and be grateful for all we have. We had to work hard for many of the things we have, or someone gave them to us and let's also remember that it's because of God that we have all that's in our life. You might think you have a good job, and you bought a lot of the things you have yet it was God that gave you that job, so you were able to buy what you needed and wanted. We need to be grateful for everything we have no matter how much or how little we have including our job and our family and friends. I learned to be grateful for another day 15 years ago when I got cancer. Now every morning I thank the Lord Jesus for giving me another day. We should be thankful for what some would call the little things which aren't little in God's eyes. What about being able to see, and talk, and hear, and walk, and even drive a car, and have food to eat. We should be thankful for the sunshine and rain and snow and bad weather as well. We might not like that it rained, and it might have messed up our plans for the day but still we need to be thankful to God for sending the weather. Afterall the rain does water our flowers and trees. God, our Creator takes care of us in more ways than we can think of because no matter what we do or where we go, God is always taking care of us. When is the last time you truly thanked God for taking care of you and even keeping you healthy because you're only healthy because the Great Physician has kept you healthy. There are so many things to be thankful for in this life and one of the big ones to be thankful for is to be thankful that you're still here because tomorrow isn't promised. Let's learn how to be more grateful for everything we have. A grateful person is a happy person because they appreciate what they have, and they don't take things for granted. Just like our tomorrows aren't promised, the material things we own aren't promised another day either because you could wreck your car and a tornado, flood, or fire could destroy your house. Be grateful for everything and be happy!

Gratitude involves taking time to look at the positive aspects of your life and appreciating what you have. It can be appreciating the people that support you in your ups and downs in life, being able to acknowledge your achievements in your career or personal life and even finding joy in little moments of your day. Learning to practice gratitude daily can give your mindset contentment even with difficulties you may face or be facing. There are many ways on how to learn to be grateful such as these.

1. Daily Reflection – just like we've been talking about, set aside a time every day to reflect on what you're grateful for and it can be something as simple as the grass or sunshine.

2. Gratitude Journal – keeping a journal for gratitude or any reason is a good thing. I have journals for a lot of different things. In your gratitude journal write down at least 3 things you're grateful for and you will see how you will start focusing on the positive things in your life.

3. Express Appreciation – show gratitude to the people around you. Thank the people for being in your life and for how they have supported you. You might be surprised how much saying thank you will help not only you but those around you.

4. Celebrate Milestones – take time to acknowledge accomplishments big and small. Thinking about how far you've come will give you a sense of gratitude.

These are just a few of the ways to incorporate a mindset of gratitude and appreciation in your overall well-being. Your mindset is what you will need to change if you are going to become truly grateful and appreciative of what you have in your life.

Showing gratitude is important for several reasons. One of the most important reasons is that it positively strengthens relationships. When you appreciate someone's kindness and show gratefulness, it will deepen your connections and will encourage more acts of kindness. Another benefit is that showing gratitude will help you to focus only on the positive aspects of your life. It will shift your perspective to looking at the present and being optimistic. It will also boost your self-esteem by giving you a positive self-image and will encourage personal growth. Showing gratitude is powerful in how it generates happiness and well-being while enriching the lives of people around you. When you have a positive self-image, that will give you a positive outlook on life and you will be more suited to face challenges that come your way. Gratitude promotes inner strength and resourcefulness, and you will be able to push any negative forces away and focus on the positive forces in your life. Gratitude also has a profound effect on our psychological well-being and promotes emotional resilience and your overall happiness is increased and your overall quality of life is improved. Gratitude also fosters feelings of self-worth and confidence. It gives us the motivation to pursue our dreams and aspirations with determination. Instead of dwelling on what we lack, gratitude helps us to focus on our blessings and opportunities that are available to us.

Gratitude is a "positive state of mind evoked by focusing on and appreciating the good in one's life; it is being conscientious about living in a state of thankfulness," according to Erin Wiley M.A., a licensed clinical psychotherapist. Gratitude can help your outlook on life by not only focusing on yourself and the blessings in your life but also the lives of others and how they have blessed you. If you practice gratitude on a regular basis, you can feel more optimistic and hopeful and be more satisfied with your life no matter how many difficulties come your way. With gratitude your perspective changes and you see things differently and you don't focus on yourself as much and you try to focus on others and their needs. With myself, it's a good feeling knowing that I can help others and that's a part of gratitude and being thankful because if you're thankful for your blessings in life, then you can bestow some of your blessings to others in your life. With everything going on in our world today, we sometimes complain more than we're being grateful and looking at the positive side. If we start practicing gratitude, we can also change not only our mindset but the way we respond to things in our world. It seems a lot easier to be grateful when things in life are going well; however, when you're facing challenges or going through difficulties, it's harder to be grateful and show acts of kindness yet the effort we put out to show gratitude will be worth it in the end. Being grateful is a choice and one that will endure in the good times and the bad. Having gratitude in your life is like giving your heart a daily dose of nourishment. You know the saying what is in your heart will show in your life so if your heart is truly grateful, then you will see it in your actions. By focusing on the positive things in your life, you show appreciation to people and experiences that bring joy to your life. People who are grateful are more compassionate, and supportive, which will lead to stronger social bonds. Gratitude will help you to have a positive outlook on life and you will be able to cope more effectively with stress and adversity. When we have a mindset of gratitude, you will nourish your heart and enhance your overall well-being. Remember your Crown is in your heart and so we need to show how grateful we are and show compassion to others. Gratitude will also give you a sense of purpose which is essential for your overall well-being. It will help you to focus on what truly matters in your life and your actions will get aligned to your values and what you value that's important. When you have gratitude and purpose in your life, then you will make choices that will help your overall health and well-being and you're better equipped to navigate difficult times with resilience and grace. You will find purpose and growth in the face of adversity. By practicing gratitude on a regular basis, you will nourish your heart by having resilience, connection, purpose, and well-being.

Gratitude is another way of saying you're thankful and both are interconnected. They both recognize and appreciate the positive aspects of your life as well as the positive relationships you have. Gratitude is a feeling of appreciation while thankfulness is the expression of gratitude. While one attribute you have as a feeling, the other you make an expression to clarify how grateful and appreciative you really are toward someone. Gratitude is where you acknowledge that your life is good and know that it's good because it comes from other sources beyond yourself. Thankfulness on the other hand is where you will actively show gratitude and appreciation and acknowledge others for their kindness and generosity. They are both interconnected because gratitude will lead to thankfulness and thankfulness will lead to gratitude. Think about it this way, you receive a gift from your friend and you're grateful that they thought enough of you to get you a gift while at the same time when you tell them thank you, you're not only acknowledging the gift but also expressing gratitude for having such a caring friend. Gratitude and thankfulness will affect your emotional and mental state and you will be able to recognize and evaluate the positive aspects of a situation while being happy and content in your resolution to the situation. Like we said earlier, your mindset is affected in almost everything you do on your journey of life, and you can train your mindset to only focus on the positive aspects of life and you will become more optimistic and have a better emotional well-being. Practicing gratitude will give you more satisfaction in your life, while also reducing stress and giving you better overall psychological well-being. Being happy and satisfied will also help you to get a better night's sleep and increase your immune system to keep you healthier. We go about our lives and do our normal routine and being grateful and thankful and trying to keep all negativity out of our lives and to only think on positive things and I'm sure if you're like me, you probably don't think about all the extra benefits you get. I hope you're beginning to see how everything we do affects our heart. You can even be happy and content when you're going through difficulties in life. That's just the way God created our bodies to work and when we're happy and content and at peace with ourselves, then our Crown will Shine through our Heart for others to see. Like I talked about earlier, what is in your heart will come out and show on the outside in our actions and emotions. So, the next time you find yourself in an ill mood, do a heart check up and see what's going on and renew your heart and spirit so others will only see love and peace and happiness coming from you. When you have the wrong attitude in your heart, it will make your Crown lay sideways and you will need to straighten it so let's keep that Crown up straight by always keeping our attitudes and emotions right in our heart and doing a heart checkup occasionally.

Matthew 15:18 says, "But those things that proceed out of the mouth come forth from the heart; and they defile the man."

So, what can being grateful and thankful do for you? It can do more than you think and if you're not being grateful maybe it's time you started. We live in a generation nowadays where people want free handouts and when all you do is get free stuff, you don't know how to be appreciative of what you have, and you don't know how to work hard to get what you might want and need. Yes, others will give you free gifts occasionally; however, I'm talking about people that don't have any idea what being grateful and appreciative is about. Those people are all too ready to take government handouts and don't want to even work and try to find a job to support themselves. People who feel entitled to get free things may struggle with gratitude because they may feel they don't need to express appreciation. Being grateful and appreciative toward others I would consider is a talent because not everyone will be grateful. You've seen people hold the door open for people at the store and it might even be raining, and some people will not even say thank you to the door holder. Even that small gesture shows how they want to help people and the least someone could do is say thank you. I understand that every person is different, and God made us all different and some people might have a hard time showing gratitude if they weren't brought up that way. I was brought up to always say thank you to anyone doing something nice such as holding open a door for me and to always be grateful for all the blessings God has bestowed on my life and in my life with the people in my life. Gratitude is a learned behavior so if you weren't brought up learning about gratitude, you will have to learn it on your own and it may be a struggle. People who have come through hardships in their life may have a hard time with gratitude because the experiences they may have faced may have made it difficult for them to recognize the positive that is in their life. Sometimes we will compare ourselves to others and I did that for a long time until I realized that we are all different and so what I do and how I act is not to be compared to anyone else's actions. Those that will try and compare themselves to others may have a hard time feeling grateful for all they have simply because someone else has more than they have, and they don't see the blessings they have in their lives, and they may only see that they're lacking compared to others that they see as having a lot of blessings. Our society and world will also play a huge role in how people look at gratitude and whether they feel grateful or not. Some people are just pessimistic and negative people, and they won't change their mindset to be positive. Whatever your reason for not showing gratitude, you can learn to be grateful through journaling, mindfulness, and acts of kindness and it will give you a more positive outlook on life. All you need to do is look around at your life and see what you do have and don't focus on what you don't have and you will see that you have a lot to be grateful for and if you start saying thank you to your friends and family for supporting you or being in your life, it can make a world of difference on your outlook on life and will eventually give you a positive mindset.

Chapter 9

COMPASSION AND FORGIVENESS

We've been talking about a lot of topics, and they all seem to be connected. Everything we deal with daily is connected to our heart and that's why we need to learn how all these different things relate to our heart so that we may keep our heart clean and pure so our Crown will stay on straight. Now we're going to talk about compassion and forgiveness and how they are connected. You need compassion to have forgiveness in your heart. How many times has someone done you wrong and you said you were not going to forgive them and did you know that by not forgiving it will hurt you more than the other person. If you hold on to unforgiveness, it can run into bitterness, and we don't need bitterness in our hearts. Now let's see what forgiveness and compassion are about. Webster defines forgiveness as, "the act of forgiving; to cease to feel resentment against, to give up resentment of or claim to requital for." Webster defines compassion as, "sympathetic consciousness of others distress together with a desire to alleviate it." Forgiveness and compassion work together because if you are a compassionate person, you will also be a forgiving person because how can you be compassionate and not be forgiving? I've had other people do me wrong and if I held on to being hateful and resentful to them for what they did or the way they acted, I couldn't be compassionate to them or to other people. Like we've been saying, it all goes along with your heart. If you have unforgiveness in your heart, then it's like having black over your heart and your Crown will not be up straight and it will not be glowing and shining for others to see. Why do you think we need to be compassionate to others anyway? What will being compassionate do for you? What does it matter if you have unforgiveness in your heart? How does God see unforgiveness? Let's dive in a little deeper and answer these questions and maybe others about compassion and forgiveness.

Don't you love it when people are compassionate to you? You're having a hard time and going through challenges and people reach out to you to offer support and may even buy groceries or whatever you may need and by people showing you compassion, it brings a smile to your face and helps you to see that others do care about you and what's going on in your life. That's what compassion is all about! It's about having our own tribe of people that we know will be there for us and with us when we face difficulties on our journey of life. God will put the people in your life that you need because He knows what your future holds, and He knows who you need to help you and encourage you. Whatever you go through in your life, remember to call out to God first to help you and He will always be there, and He will send people your way and He will comfort your heart and give you peace and wisdom and understanding over whatever you're facing. Don't ever think you don't need God or anyone and that you can handle it all on your own, because you can't. Things can get rough when you try to tackle things all on your own and without God, you will be without blessings in your life that only God will bestow to you. I've heard people say before that they don't need anyone and that they're fine by themselves, yet they don't realize what they are even saying because we all need interaction with other people and our world is made up of social interaction. That's why compassion is a key factor in our lives because of the social interaction that we face every day. Compassion will give us deeper relationships with others whether it is family, friends, or even strangers that God may put in our path to help us. When you feel understood and supported, it makes you feel good, and you will pass the torch as the saying goes to help someone else. We've talked a lot about our emotional well-being earlier and compassion also affects our emotional well-being in that it will extend positive emotions to us. When someone shows you kindness, you will feel emotions of happiness, and a sense of purpose. Have you ever been depressed and felt like you couldn't go on, well I have, and when someone showed kindness to me or helped me in any way, it gave me a sense of purpose and it helped me to get back on the right track in life. Improved emotional health through being compassionate will give you an improved mood, lower your stress, as well as give you improved mental health. By showing compassion to others, we can help to alleviate any hardship or pain. We can help others and give them a sense of hope simply by showing them compassion. Have you ever had someone have a death or some catastrophe and you brought them food or sent them flowers and a card, well that did more than you think because just knowing someone cares will make your heart happy. I've lost several friends and family over the past few years and when I got a text or a card in the mail, it put a smile on my face, and it helped me to press on through the difficulty.

Compassion will also build trust between people because when you're compassionate toward someone and they're going through challenges and difficulties, they feel valued and supported and most to the time will be more open to communicate what challenges they are facing. Being compassionate will promote harmony and unity between people because now there is a connection. When we're showing compassion, we not only help ourselves, but we also help others because we are giving a part of ourselves to others in showing that we care and offering support to whatever difficulty they might be facing. There have been times that I helped someone going through a hard time and I might not really know them, and they were just an acquaintance yet after I showed compassion and they saw that I truly cared, we became friends and so we can also be an encouragement to others through compassion. When you practice compassion, you will see personal growth in yourself, and your mindset will see qualities such as patience and humility. I must admit I have never been much of a patient person yet over the years as I've been helping more people, I've seen that I have become more patient and that is due to personal growth in myself. You will be able to see personal growth and development as you start showing compassion and helping others. I hope you're beginning to see that being compassionate not only helps the other person but also helps you. It will encourage you to expand your perspective and your self-awareness will help you to see others needs and be willing to helping others when you can. By having compassion in our interactions and behaviors, we not only enhance other people's lives but also improve our own lives in many ways. So why is it important to show compassion to others? It's one way to enrich your life and to grow your personal life and mindset while also making our world more compassionate and encouraging others. By focusing on the needs and challenges of others, you're also able to look at your own challenges and face them with resilience. By focusing on other's needs, your brain will release feelings of pleasure and send you calmness and relaxation. You will also be able to possess a more positive outlook on life. Compassion overall will give you a sense of purpose and fulfillment as you continue to help others and make a positive impact in their lives.

Now let's talk about forgiveness and see how it's connected to compassion. Forgiveness as we said earlier is the ability to let go of resentment against someone that has done you wrong. You might even say you're not talking to that person ever again, and believe me, I understand that feeling because I've said it too yet that's not the right approach to take. When I realized that God was not happy with my response, then I began to realize that I can't be the happy person I am without letting go of all the anger I had in my heart. We talked about negative influences on our life earlier and by not showing forgiveness, you are allowing negativity in your life because unforgiveness is holding on to a negative emotion. Forgiveness does not necessarily mean forgetting about the wrong that has been done yet you are freeing yourself from holding on to negative emotions that will affect your overall body. Forgiveness allows you to move forward with your life without dwelling on hurt and resentment and other negative emotions and to find peace within yourself. We've talked about stress before and if you hold on to unforgiveness, it will also give you unneeded stress as well as other health issues so by showing forgiveness, you will be able to reduce your stress levels and help other to improve your overall health. Compassion and forgiveness are connected, and one leads to the other because when you forgive, you can show compassion and understanding. You can have compassion without first forgiving because forgiveness may come later if you need a lot of healing. Compassion is understanding, recognizing, and responding to the suffering of others while forgiveness involves letting go of all your anger and resentment. You can have compassion without forgiveness because forgiveness is an emotional journey that may take some time to heal. When you're hurt in the heart and your heart is broken in pieces because of your husband's desire to break up your marriage, then that will take awhile to get over and I know how emotional that is because I went through that. God was the one in that hurt and pain that healed my heart and He put a new person in my life that made me smile again. No matter what you're going through, even if you can't show forgiveness to that person, you can still show compassion to others and in so doing, it will help you in the long run and with God's help, you will be able to heal.

Now, let's see what God thinks about forgiveness because we've looked at why we need to forgive and that is simply because it harms our body not to and we don't need negative forces in our body and mindset. God says that if we don't forgive others, then He won't forgive us and we all know that we sin every second of every minute of every hour of every day that we're on this earth, so we need God's forgiveness, and He is the God of many chances. God is the Bigger Picture so we should want God to forgive us and that's the main reason why we should forgive. I'm sure you've seen people like I have, and you can see by their expression that they're holding something in their heart, and when you don't forgive, it will lead to bitterness and that is something that others will see from your appearance and actions. God is merciful and gracious to us and is always forgiving and He even sent His Son Jesus Christ to die on the cruel cross of Calvary and rose again to pay for all our sins. We have a forgiving God and if you have Jesus in your heart, then you know how forgiving God is so we should have a forgiving heart and I do understand that sometimes it's hard to forgive. Take time to heal if you have something hurtful and painful but, in the end, Forgive and go on with your life. Forgiveness reflects the true nature and character of God so we should strive to be more like God and be as forgiving as we possibly can. We shouldn't have any unforgiveness in our hearts and if we do, we should ask ourselves why and seek to find ways to forgive whoever did us wrong. Forgiveness is essential for healing relationships and restoring harmony. If we choose to not forgive, it will be harmful to your spiritual well-being and like it says In Matthew 6:14, "For if you forgive others for their transgressions, your Heavenly Father will also forgive you." Unforgiveness is a barrier to your prayer life because Jesus said that if you have unforgiveness in your heart, He will not hear your prayers. When we leave this earth, we will all be judged for every action and every spoken word, so wouldn't you rather not have unforgiveness in your heart so that you won't be judged on why you didn't forgive someone? Holding on to unforgiveness can lead to bitterness like we talked about earlier and it can also lead to resentment and emotional bondage because you can't experience the freedom and peace that will come from forgiving others so you're keeping your emotional well-being in jail and not free to feel all the happy feelings if you would show forgiveness. We all want the best life, and we want to live the best life so how can we do that with unforgiveness in our hearts. So, I hope you see that unforgiveness is harmful to your spiritual life as well as your emotional well-being because it hinders personal growth and harmony. Also remember your Crown will have a hard time staying straight in your heart if all you have is unforgiveness. Your Crown thrives in happy, peaceful, joyful, and loving attributes in your heart. Forgiveness is a transformative attribute as it not only shows our relationship with God, but it also shows our relationship with others. As you're showing compassion to others, allow yourself to release all the negative forces over your heart and emotions, and show forgiveness.

Compassion and forgiveness are both essential in our lives to not only help others but to help ourselves. If we have them in our lives, they will promote well-being in our life as well as others lives, and we will have healthy relationships and have more harmony and inner peace in our lives. When we are compassionate toward others struggles and challenges and at the same time, forgiving of mistakes, it strengthens our relationships with everyone. Those with compassionate hearts seem to have higher emotional intelligence where they can understand and manage their own emotions more effectively and they will also understand the needs of others and see how they can help them through their difficulties in life. Being compassionate and forgiving will also help you to bounce back quicker from setbacks and adversities and you will also find constructive solutions to conflicts that come your way. While compassion is seeing the needs of others and understanding how to help them through their challenges, forgiveness is self-reflection where you must look within yourself and be willing to let go of past hurts which will give you an increase in self-awareness and maturity for any obstacles that will come. Compassion and forgiveness are essential to resolve conflicts peacefully because you might need someone to be compassionate toward you to help you understand how to resolve a conflict and then you will be willing to forgive someone that hurt you and go on peacefully with your journey of life. The attributes of compassion and forgiveness are essential to both the giver and the taker because as you're helping someone with their difficulty in life, you also have a sense of purpose and fulfillment while you're helping someone in need.

Chapter 10
FINDING PURPOSE

◇◇

We talked in the last chapter a little bit about how being compassionate and forgiving will give you a purpose in life. So, what is your purpose and what is our purpose on our journey of life? Why do we need purpose in life? I'm sure if you're like me, you have thought about purpose and what is your reason for being on this earth. First and foremost, I do know that we're on this earth to spread the Good News Gospel to everyone. If you don't know what I'm talking about, it's the Lord Jesus Christ that died on the cruel cross of Calvary and rose again the 3rd day to pay for our sins so that we might be with Him forever in Heaven one day. Those of us who have Jesus in our hearts will go to Heaven when we leave this earth, and if you don't have Jesus in your heart, all you need to do is ask Him to forgive you and repent of your sins and ask Him to save you and come into your heart. That's the main purpose of life and there are other things about purpose we will talk about. Webster defines purpose as, "something set up as an object or end; a subject under discussion or an action in course of execution." So, according to Webster's definition our purpose is something that we do or are planning on doing. If God has called you to be a pastor or like myself, called you to write faith books, then that is your purpose. You can have many purposes in this life because you might have many talents and skills where you are able to help others by doing many things. You could be a writer and you could also have your own business where you're helping others in your community with your business and in that respect, you do have more than one purpose in life. My main purpose is to tell others about Jesus and then to listen as He speaks to me and write faith books. I guess seeking God's will for your life could also be another word for purpose. It is basically the same because God does have a will for your life, and He already has it planned out what you will do in this life, yet most people call it their purpose in life and not God's will even though most Christians will say God's will for their life. Whether you call it purpose or God's will, it will take you looking within yourself and asking God what your purpose on this earth is and seeing what your values, interests, and passions are. You might love making things for the elderly so you may think about opening a shop to help the elderly and widowed in your town. If you don't already have a purpose in your life, then you might want to see what it is that your heart loves and go from there. There are plenty of ways to find what your purpose is and we're going to talk about a few of them.

1. Identify Your Strengths – what are you good at, what are your interests, what do you love doing? Your purpose may be to utilize the abilities that you already have.

2. Set Goals – set long-term and short-term goals that relate to your interests. This will give you direction as you work toward achieving your goals.

3. Explore Opportunities – explore new experiences, hobbies, or career paths, take classes, or even travel. You can expand your

perspective by getting out of your comfort zone and trying something new.

Finding your purpose in life isn't hard and it can also be fun because you might find that you love doing something that you didn't know before. If it is something new that you haven't done before, you can also watch videos on how other people are doing the same thing and get your perspective on how you want to do it yet doing it your way. Finding a purpose in your life is always a challenge and will have its ups and downs so just look at them as opportunities for learning and growth. You will need persistence and resilience as you find your purpose because as you grow so will your purpose. Remember to have gratitude for opportunities and experiences because gratitude will help you to stay grounded and connected to what truly matters as you find your purpose in your journey of life. Finding purpose is a process that will evolve over time, and it won't happen overnight so be patient and open to new opportunities that God will send your way. Remember to always be asking God to show you the correct direction and pathway that you should take.

When we hear people talk about purpose, most are looking for the reason for their existence on earth and what they're supposed to be doing while they're here. Purpose is the reasoning as to our existence. It gives our life direction, fulfillment, and significance. Think about driving your car and you have no idea where you're going and you're just driving and, in that scenario, you have no direction and having purpose is the same thing because if you don't have a purpose in life, then you will be floating down life doing this and that and not having any reason why you do anything. Having purpose will give you a clear sense of direction and meaning in life. When we have a purpose, we know what we're aiming for, and we know what we need to focus on. Purpose will help us to set and have meaningful goals in life and we will feel connected and when we're connected, we will be more committed. We will also have a sense of fulfillment because as we age, we want to know that we have a purpose in life and have something to keep us motivated and knowing that our actions matter, and we can also having an impact on people's lives will give you satisfaction. Having a purpose in life will help us to reflect on our legacy and what mark we will be leaving in this world. Having a purpose in life provides us with direction, motivation, and a sense of fulfillment and will enrich all areas of our life as we go on our journey of life. Purpose will guide your life decisions, offer a sense of direction as well as influence your behaviors and give your life more meaning. Purpose will give you stability and a sense of direction and will give you a happy and healthy life. With purpose to your life, you will make your life more meaningful, and you will know where you're coming from and where you are going. Your emotional and mental energy is what will drive your purpose because it is full of all the emotions of excitement and happiness. Your purpose will inspire you to reach for big dreams. Other people can even encourage you to reach for those dreams and help you to obtain your purpose in life. Purpose will help you guide life decisions, shape your goals, and create meaningful life experiences. People with a purpose know what they want out of life, and they know how to reach their goals. Having a purpose will guide you and give you a sense of direction and stability. Finding a purpose in your life is essential to having a happy and healthy life. Not that you couldn't have a healthy and happy life without purpose; however, it could be much happier because you will have direction and stability.

Finding purpose in life is different for each person because we're all different and learning to live your life with purpose will give you a sense of control and contentment. Feeling like what you do has a meaning and is worthwhile is a key for a happy life. To find purpose in your life, you will need to do self-reflection and look within yourself and see what you love to do and see what your attributes are. A lot of people seem to say they want to find a purpose in life, yet most don't want to spend the time or effort it takes to find their purpose in life. It will take work and it will take time. Like we said earlier, purpose of life is an individual process because each person has different interests and skills. To find your purpose in life, you will need to grow your mindset and grow and become a better you. As you grow your mindset, you will be able to see challenges more as opportunities for growth and even when failures come your way, you will be able to accept it. You can create a personal vision statement and that would be like the new year's resolutions that most people do in January and that can be your roadmap to guide you in the direction you want to go. With a roadmap you will see what is important to you and it will make it easier for you to make decisions based on your values. You might try giving back where you help others in need to find your sense of purpose. You can spread kindness simply by doing random acts of kindness. We talked about gratitude before and gratitude is also connected to finding purpose in the sense that as you show gratitude and show acts of kindness, it will contribute to your finding a sense of purpose. We've all gone through some sort of pain in our lives, and you can turn your pain into a purpose by helping others to overcome the same kind of pain you went through. If you spend time with people who are positive and purpose driven, they can inspire you and you can train your mindset to be positive and purpose driven, and you will find your purpose in life. Make sure to also make time for self-care as that is important in finding your purpose. Relax your brain and have some creative thinking and it will get you closer to finding your purpose.

You don't want to always be on autopilot on your journey in this life and finding your purpose isn't that hard. Like I said earlier, I found my purpose to be writing books and before I did that, I had several author friends and I was reading their books and I was getting inspiration from them and then God gave me the green light and told me I needed to start writing and that has put me at peace from day one knowing that I was doing something meaningful. Purpose gives you a compass for your life and guides you with every decision and experience. Purpose gives us all a meaning in life and a reason for why we do what we do. With purpose driven lives, we will pursue goals that are like our values and passions as well as contributing to the well-being of others. Finding purpose involves self-discovery and looking within ourselves and finding our true values and beliefs and connecting with others along the way to inspire and encourage us. I hope you're beginning to see that finding purpose in our lives is important unless we want to be on autopilot all our lives and it is personal to everyone because each person will have a different purpose based on their interests and skills and what they love to do. There are many ways that you can find purpose in your life and one way is to reflect on your values and beliefs. Take the time to see what matters the most to you and seeing what your values are will give you an understanding of what direction you need to go to find your purpose. Pay attention to your hobbies and interests and by exploring your passions you will see what areas in your life that you can find purpose and fulfillment. Pay attention to your inner voice and trust yourself to make decisions based on your values. Don't pay attention to all the outside voices that will try and tell you what you can and can't do and listen to what your heart tells you and to what your instincts tell you as to the direction you need to go in finding purpose in your life. You know what you love to do and what makes you happy and no one else will be able to tell you which direction you should be going. Stay open to new opportunities, new possibilities and experiences that may come your way and above all trust yourself to make the right choices that are meaningful and true to yourself.

In trying to find purpose and meaning in your life, look for things in your daily life that already brings you joy and pleasure. As we go through our life, we have things we do daily that will lead us to find purpose and so take notice of ordinary moments in life which could be something as simple as working on your car. You might find purpose in helping others with their automotive problems. You need to take care of yourself while searching for your purpose with self-care and self-compassion. Take time to rest, recharge, and engage in activities that will help you energize your mind, body, and soul. We talked about being compassionate toward others and we also need to be compassionate and kind to ourselves because sometimes life gets rough, and we need to stop and rest. If you're already pursuing a purpose driven life, remember to celebrate your progress and achievements. Acknowledge your success and milestones no matter how big or small and by celebrating your achievements, it will help you to stay motivated. Always believe in your ability to create a purposeful life that has meaning and is fulfilling and is geared toward who you are and have faith in your journey of life that lies ahead. Practice mindfulness and keep your mindset geared toward growing and improving to become a better you. Pay attention to the present moment in your daily life and stay aware and in tune with your inner self. Mindfulness will help you with intuition, desires, and aspirations and it will lead you to understanding your purpose. You can also get in tune with nature and get a sense of peace and inspiration even if it's just a walk around the neighborhood. I take a walk in our huge 2 acres and sometimes even walk around the neighborhood to get clarity on something or just to refresh my brain. There are many ways to find inspiration and you can even go to the mountains or ocean and get inspiration so find what works for you to find inspiration. Always stay open to life's new experiences, and ideas and see what new directions you will be able to go down. Allow yourself to be creative and have spontaneity and imagination and rediscover your joy. Purpose is not a set destination; it is a journey of growth and self-discovery. Your sense of purpose may evolve and change over time as you grow and learn and experience life. There is a process of self-discovery in finding purpose in this life and I've had several things in my lifetime that I thought was my purpose and the more my mindset was growing, the more my purpose in life would change. Acknowledge the value you have in your unique gifts and remember that each person has their own set of unique gifts and not one person has the same set of unique gifts. Take each step of your journey with courage and a sense of adventure knowing that with each step, you will be getting closer to living a life of purpose, meaning, and fulfillment.

Chapter 11

CELEBRATING VICTORIES

〜〜〜〜〜〜〜〜〜〜〜〜〜〜〜〜〜〜〜〜〜〜〜

As we travel on our journey of life, sometimes our life is hard and sometimes it's easy yet when we have accomplished our goals and successes, we need to celebrate how far we have come. You better believe when I became bestselling author on Amazon, I celebrated and told everyone I could. There is something special about celebrating our victories because no matter what they are and no matter how long it took for us to get there, we did it. So next time you accomplish a goal or even a dream, don't think that it's something small because no matter if you think it's small, someone else will see it as a big accomplishment. The fact that you did it and didn't give up is a big accomplishment and God helped you get to where you are now. As you celebrate your successes, don't forget to be grateful and thank those who were there helping you and supporting you. I remember years ago, I was so shy and quict, and I wouldn't dare have a conversation with someone I didn't know, and now I talk to anyone I see, and I even talk on podcasts with strangers about my books. That's a big accomplishment for me and to some they might think that's not a big deal and that I probably just came out of my shell. It's more than that because God helped me to see that I have a story and a testimony, and I need to be talking to everyone and inspiring and encouraging people. Be proud of how far you have come and with what you have accomplished. Now let's look at the definition of victories and see why we need to celebrate victories. What kind of victories can you have? Why should you tell others what you have accomplished? Webster defines victory as, "the overcoming of an enemy or antagonist; achievement of mastery or success in a struggle or endeavor against odds or difficulties." You can have victories in all aspects of your life from personal, professional, academic, and social. Personal victories can include overcoming a phobia like public speaking or like myself being an introvert and afraid to talk to people. Personal victories can also include personal growth such as learning a new skill or overcoming a personal struggle such as a mental health issue. Professional victories can include getting a job promotion or even getting recognition for outstanding performance at your job. Another professional victory could be starting and growing your own business. Academic victories could include graduating with honors and even overcoming academic challenges. Social victories can include building and maintaining strong relationships with friends and family, having a positive impact in your community by volunteering, and overcoming shyness as I talked about how that was one of my victories. No matter what kind of victory you have accomplished, it shows that you had personal growth and you had determination to get it done. Any victory will take perseverance, dedication, and even stepping out of your comfort zone. Celebrating the victories in your life can also boost your confidence and overall well-being.

Celebrating your victories is important because it shows other people how far you have come and how you have grown in your overall well-being. It will make you proud to be telling or showing others about your successes. It acknowledges to others all the hard work, perseverance, and motivation that it took for you to accomplish your success. It will give you a positive environment where you can have continued success and growth. When you celebrate victories, you can reflect on the progress you've made and see how far you have come, and you will know what you can do with dedication and motivation. With victory celebrations, you can recognize the effort, dedication, and the hard work that had to be accomplished to get the work done. It provides a sense of accomplishment and satisfaction and encourages you to keep continuing for success in the future. Celebrations will give you a positive atmosphere and it will give you a sense of unity and strengthen bonds with others. We talked earlier about how having positive forces around you are good and that negative forces aren't good so anytime you have victories in life, you need to celebrate them to keep the positive forces in your life. There is reflection when you celebrate victories because you will see what worked and what didn't, and it will help future outcomes. We've talked a lot about how certain things we do will encourage others as well as encourage us, and celebrating victories will also encourage others to pursue their own goals with determination. Any victory that you have should be celebrated whether you consider it small or big because it gives you an opportunity to acknowledge progress toward bigger goals you have in the future. Small or big victories will contribute to your overall success in your journey of life. It will also have an impact on your mental and emotional well-being because it will boost your confidence and promote a sense of accomplishment. Celebrating victories is not just about the outcome but also about the journey and all the motivation, determination, and the hard work that was involved.

You might think that other people won't care about what you have accomplished; however, you are incorrect because we should all care about the successes of our family, friends, and coworkers. Anytime someone is celebrating a victory, it should encourage others to strive to do their best and be determined to accomplish the goals they have in their life. Celebrating victories is also essential for maintaining a positive and productive mindset. It's a reminder of all the progress made and the goals achieved and is motivating to others, especially during difficult and challenging times. Our world is made up of social interaction so when you celebrate your victories, it affects the psychological aspect of all those involved. When you see your efforts turn into successes, it reinforces in your mind that your actions can lead to positive outcomes and all your hard work has paid off. It's a renewed motivation to keep you and those around you encouraged and to keep going to achieve their goals. It's beneficial when you're going through difficult times, and you can be reminded that you need to keep going and stay motivated to get the goal achieved. By celebrating victories, you will feel valued, motivated, and empowered to pursue your goals and it not only acknowledges past achievements but can also inspire future goals encouraging continued growth and success. Our world is made up of social interaction so by celebrating victories, you will be interacting with others and encouraging and motivating them to pursue their goals and obtain their own victories. Anytime there is a victory celebration, it will motivate you and give you a surge of confidence to go even higher to accomplish a bigger goal because you will feel empowered to push the boundaries and tackle new challenges. It will also promote a growth mindset and we've been talking about how anything that we do is affected by our mindset. So, we need to keep growing our mindset to keep going higher and higher and being able to move out of our comfort zone more easily. We need to shift our mindset away from where it was originally to obtain the mindset where we view any setbacks and obstacles as a learning and growing experience instead of failures or losses and we will continue with determination to pursue our goals. When we acknowledge and celebrate victories along our way, we will stay motivated and determined to stay focused on the objective. Celebrating victories is not just about praising accomplishments, it's about appreciation and resilience that will benefit people, organizations, and the world we live in. Each victory that we accomplish is a testament to our resilience and we keep moving forward with renewed determination. Victories will give us solace, accomplishment, and determination to keep moving forward one step at a time toward our journey of growth and will give us strength for the future victories to come.

Celebrating our victories is important for a lot of reasons and the main reason being that by acknowledging our wins, we will reinforce belief in ourselves and our abilities. We recognize our strengths, and we are proud for what we have accomplished and for how far we have come. It makes us feel more optimistic because we can see that we can overcome challenges we face and achieve our goals. Celebrating every success will boost our self-esteem and will give us a positive self-image. Like we talked about earlier, it doesn't have to be a celebration for a big victory because we need to celebrate the small victories as well because they are steppingstones to the bigger victories. Celebrating victories is important because it reinforces positive behavior and encourages us to continue to have more success. It will give you confidence which will lead to a sense of accomplishment. As you celebrate victories, it will allow you to look back and reflect on how far you have come to see what you have accomplished, and you will appreciate all the hard work you had to go through to get where you are now on your journey of life. It contributes to a healthier and more fulfilling personal and professional life. While we are celebrating our victories, our brain is also at work because it affects the psychological aspect of our bodies by releasing the dopamine in the brain which gives us feelings of pleasure and satisfaction. It helps us to feel good in the moment and to believe in our abilities to succeed. Celebrating victories will also add meaning to our lives by recognizing and honoring achievements. It will help us to reflect on the journey we took in our life to get where we are now and remember the challenges and obstacles we faced and overcame, and the moments of growth and learning that were accomplished as we reached our goal. It will help us to see valuable insights into ourselves and see our strengths, weaknesses, and areas for improvement. It will affect our emotional well-being as it will give us joy and satisfaction and boost our mood. The emotional aspect will have a lasting effect giving us resilience and optimism for future challenges. Celebrating victories is all about creating moments for joy, connection, and reflection that will inspire us to keep reaching new heights in the future. We've been talking about victories and what kinds of victories we can have and why we need to celebrate them, yet we haven't defined what celebrating means. Webster defines celebrate as, "to perform publicly and with appropriate rites; to honor; to mark by festivities." So, when we celebrate our victories both small and big, we are marking them as something out of the ordinary and something to pay attention to because it was a lot of hard work and determination, and motivation to get this accomplished and you are wanting everyone to know how proud you are of yourself for how far you have come. A sense of accomplishment over your success in life will keep you going because you will get a high energy rush over it. Happiness is the joy of achievement, and the human spirit needs to accomplish and triumph to be happy. Happiness isn't found from doing easy everyday work, it comes from satisfaction after the work is done and after the achievement of a difficult task that demanded all your hard work and energy. Happiness comes at the realization that you have accomplished something.

Motivation is a key to success and sometimes you find it hard to stay motivated; however, your brain is what fuels motivation because it will release dopamine and give us a sense of pleasure when we accomplish something, and this encourages us to repeat the behavior in the future. Motivation is also regulated by the prefrontal cortex and limbic system, and they regulate your emotions for decision making and so they play a more essential role in what motivates us. Dopamine and serotonin are the neurotransmitters that play a vital role in motivating us to do certain tasks. When this is released from the brain, we will feel a sense of pleasure as well as satisfaction. Even the thought of achieving something pleasurable will provide motivation. Another neurotransmitter called norepinephrine will affect our motivational levels by producing alertness in response to any stressors or challenges we face. Motivation will provide the energy you need to pursue and accomplish the goal and when the goal is achieved, your brain will release even more dopamine which will give us feelings of happiness, pride, and satisfaction that we have accomplished our goal. Our brain will accelerate with dopamine as we perceive success to be closer. So, in celebrating our victories, our brain is also involved in the process of staying motivated and determined to get the goal accomplished. God created our bodies in such a way that our brain knows when we are getting close to achieving our goal and so will release more chemicals and that is what gives us the sense of happiness and achievement. The next time you are working toward a goal and you're almost at the end of finishing it, notice that you start getting excited that it's almost done and that's your brain sending chemicals your way. Isn't that just exciting to know God created your brain in such a way as to know when we need the sensation of excitement and happiness as well as satisfaction as we reach our goals.

When you celebrate victories, your brain will release neurotransmitters to give you a sense of pleasure and reward. This will create positive emotions and will motivate you to achieve more successes in the future. Celebrating victories can also reduce stress and promote overall well-being. Celebrating victories gives you the feelings of accomplishment and when you achieve something momentum, your brain will see it as competence. This will boost your confidence and self-esteem and it will motivate you to strive for more success. You will also receive positive emotions and those will counter act any negative emotions so celebrating victories will not only uplift your mood but also give you a sense of optimism and improve your overall emotional well-being. Celebrations will provide you with a sense of closure and acknowledgement for how far you have come and for all your hard work. It shapes our attitudes, behaviors, and perceptions as we appreciate and acknowledge our accomplishments in celebrating our victories. Celebrating victories has a profound effect on your overall personal growth and well-being in that your mindset now knows how capable you are to accomplish a goal with challenges, and you will have more positive forces driving you with your brain helping to send chemicals when it senses you are completing a goal. So, no matter what you're trying to do in your life, remember your brain is equipped in such a way to help you along the way as you tackle challenges. Get out there and celebrate all those accomplishments and successes!

Chapter 12

UNWAVERING FAITH, TRUSTING
THE GREATER PLAN

We have been talking about a lot of things that will affect your heart and that will try and knock at your Crown to keep it from being straight in your heart. We've also talked about how we can celebrate our victories and thus keep our Crown on straight in our heart and I hope you see how your brain will also affect how you achieve things on your journey of life. As you're navigating challenges on your journey of life, it is your heart that you must keep pure and clean so your Crown will sit up proudly and straight. There will be times in our lives where we need to do a heart checkup and ask God to clean your heart from bad attitudes and other things that don't need to be in there. We talked at the beginning that this is just part of the bigger picture, the greater plan. Keeping our heart clean so our Crown will stay up straight will require you to have faith and trust in God and trust that God will help you in times of challenges and difficulties. Jesus Christ and Faith is the greater plan and it's all a part of us and our journey of life. We don't know what will happen tomorrow because we can't see the future, yet God already knows because He's already there. We might say we are going to do something tomorrow but when you say that you need to say God willing, I will do that because you never know what will happen. So, who are you trusting? Do you trust the Greater Plan or something else? Where is your faith and who are you trusting in? What is unwavering faith? These are a few of the questions we will answer. Webster's definition of unwavering is, "continuing in a strong and steady way," and his definition for faith is, "allegiance to duty or a person; belief and trust in and loyalty to God." So unwavering faith is staying strong in believing and trusting in God and the Greater Plan. It is to have the confidence we talked about earlier that will respond to any challenges with immediate obedience. In essence, it means to have trust and faith in God that He and only He will take care of the situation and work it out for the best. This means to not try and "fix" a situation on your own because God is already at work and His plans will work 10 times better than any of our plans. Jeremiah 29:11 says, "for I know the plans I have for you, declares the Lord, plans to prosper you and not to harm you, plans to give you hope and a future."

So, what is the Greater Plan and why do we need to have faith in it? The Greater Plan is the plan that God has for all our lives, and it is guided by God's love for us and His wisdom and Him being the Sovereign God. Even in our lives when we go through tough times, challenges, and difficulties, we can trust that God will be there for us and will never forsake us. Before you will be able to trust and have faith in God, you need to know God and His Son Jesus Christ. If you don't know Jesus, He died on the cruel cross of Calvary and rose again the 3rd day to pay for all our sins and all you need to do is repent and ask Jesus to come into your heart and then you will become a new person because you will have Jeus in your heart. When we have

Jesus in our heart, then He gives us a Crown to wear because we are a Child of The King as I mentioned earlier, and we need to keep our Crown straight in our heart to show others the love of Jesus in our heart. We have a testimony and others are watching us and our testimony and so we need to let our Crown shine and be straight in our heart for others to see. Our trust and faith should be in Jesus and stay strong and constant; however, I know there are times when it's hard to have constant faith when our lives are going through difficulties. I've been there and there were times where my faith was struggling and so I had to pray to God to help me to increase my faith and He did just that. Trust in God and He will give you the peace that passes all understanding and it's a peace that no man can understand. Not having strong faith is like what we have been talking about when how we act or speak knocks at our Crown trying to make it go sideways in our Heart. So, if we can get our actions and attitudes right so that we can keep our Crown straight, then I think we can keep our faith strong and trust only in God to help us. Satan is all the time trying to tempt you and throw things your way and even use people in your pathway to make you stumble; however, if you fully trust in God, there isn't anything that Satan or this world can do to you. You are God's Child and He created you and He will take care of you. So, in your happy times trust God and in times of uncertainty and difficulty, you can really trust and believe God because He will not let you down. People will let you down, but God won't let you down. Psalms 118:8 says, "It is better to take refuge in the Lord than to trust in man."

So, how can we have unwavering faith in God and trust the Greater Plan? The number one way to have unwavering faith in God is prayer and reading God's Word, the Bible because when you pray, you talk to God, and when you read the Bible, God speaks to you. What better way to get constant and unwavering faith than to talk to God and listen to God talk to you. He will speak to you and give you wisdom and understanding and give you directions. This is the number one way to strengthen your relationship with God and trust in His plan. The Bible will also give you insight into God's character, His promises, and His plan as you read about Him, and it will increase your faith. If you accept that God's ways and God's plans are better than yours and let go and surrender your life to Him, you will see your faith increase. God has always been faithful to you, and you can look back and see how He took care of you and as you look back, you will see how He loves and cares for you. I'm sure there has been times when you had to wait on God to perform His plan on your life and so remember that God's timing isn't like our timing. Trust God's plans as you wait for Him to fulfil His plan in your life. Even if you can't see things happening, God is working out the situation for you because He is putting everything in place. There have been times in my life where I didn't know what God was doing because I didn't see anything happening and with us being human, we always want it done immediately yet it's in God's time and He knows the future and He knows what must be set up before He can move and take care of your situation. Another way to trust God's plan is to show gratitude like we talked about earlier. Thank God for all the blessings He has bestowed on your life and while you're thanking Him, you will shift your focus away from your difficulty and challenge and focus more on God and how good He has been to you. Be obedient to God's commands and this will increase your faith. Obedience will demonstrate your trust in God and His wisdom and authority over your life. Trusting in God's plans will require letting go of pride and submitting to His wisdom and guidance. Focus on the attributes of God which includes love, faithfulness, and goodness and reminding yourself who God is will strengthen your faith in Him and you will trust and have faith in God's plan for you and your life. Whatever challenges and difficulties come your way, remember that you're just passing through on this earth to a better place in Heaven with Jesus. Trusting in the Greater Plan is believing in His promise of eternal life and Him fulfilling His promises in your life.

As you grow in your spiritual journey, you will increase your faith and trust in God and His Greater Plan, and you will start to have a steadfast faith in the purposes for your life. Don't try and have control, leave all the control of your life to God. Take all your worries and cares to God daily and you will start to see how He is working in your life. The Holy Spirit lives within you and so let Him provide you comfort, wisdom, and assurance when you're going through difficulties and challenges in your life and that will help you to trust in God's plan. Keeping a prayer journal will help to increase your faith and you will have unwavering faith because you will write down all your prayer requests as well as experiences and the many ways God has helped and been faithful to you. Understand that uncertainty in life is just a part of life and trust that God will always be present even in the middle of uncertainties of life. With this understanding, you are surrendering your control and relying on God's guidance and wisdom. I'm not saying just sit down and let God do everything when you have challenges in life because you still need to pray to God and ask for wisdom and direction and sometimes you might need to do something for God to work out your specific situation. With unwavering faith, you will be in constant prayer to God and seeing what He needs you to do. There have been times I was waiting on God to help me, and He told me I needed to do something and then when I obeyed God's voice then the difficulty was taken care of with God's plan. Trust the Greater Plan and trust that God will always take care of you and whatever you're facing in life. You need to also be aware of your mindfulness and always be mindful of God speaking to you in that still small voice and sometimes you will need to get rid of distractions to hear His voice. Mindfulness will help you to have faith in God's plan and you will see His hand at work. Remember how we were talking about your mindset and how you need to grow your mindset to keep you Crown on straight, well you also need to keep your mindfulness where you will be attentive to God when He speaks to you. I've heard people say before that they pray and don't get any answers and my response to them is are you truly listening for God's voice because if you don't get to where you can hear it, He will speak to your heart, and you won't be paying attention. The things in this world are so distracting that if we try to listen for God's voice, we might not hear it unless we get away from all the world's distractions. Even with writing books, sometimes I need peace and quiet to get inspiration from God as to what needs to be written in my books. With unwavering faith and trusting God's plan, you will get to the point to where you will be able to recognize God's voice and you will trust only in Him.

Always think about your spiritual well-being like you do your physical well-being. You need to grow your spiritual well-being just like your overall physical well-being. You can obtain spiritual growth through Bible study, prayer, and fellowship with other believers. As you get a stronger relationship with God, you will get a better understanding of His plan for your life, and you will grow in your faith as you trust in God. Trust in God's promises and keep your faith in God's promises as assurances for what He can do in your life. Another thing to grow your faith is by practicing forgiveness like we were talking about earlier because God forgave you of your sins and you should forgive others when they do you wrong and hurt you. Being able to discern God's voice and direction is available through prayer and studying the Bible and it will help you to align your decisions and actions in life with God's plans.

Testify to others how God has been faithful in your life. We all have a testimony of faith and when we share our testimony, we are showing that we have God's love in our hearts. Let others see how God has answered your prayers and how He has protected and strengthened you and by doing so, that will strengthen your own faith and it will also encourage others to trust God's Plan. Lean on God and trust Him completely to get you through trials and certainties you will face. You will be able to increase your faith and trust in God's Greater Plan and experience peace and guidance in every aspect of your life as you go on your journey of life. When you're going through difficulties and challenges, always seek God's will and purpose for what is going on in your life. Sometimes God will grow your spiritualty through difficulties and hardships in your life. God can always use difficult circumstances for your growth, transformation, and His glory. We've been talking about always reflecting on what's within yourself and even with having unwavering faith, you need to have self-reflection. You need to look and recognize the ways God has been at work in your life and by doing self-reflection and remembering how God has been faithful and encouraged you in the past, it will help you to strengthen your faith and to keep trusting in God and His plan. Trusting God's plan also includes being open to what God wants you to do and sometimes that will mean stepping out of your comfort zone to do what God wants you to do. All God is doing when He asks you to step out of your comfort zone is shaping you into the person, He created you to be. Rather than being overcome with the difficulties in your life, trust that God will use them to refine your character to increase your faith in Him and His Great Plan. There's no need to worry when you have God and your faith is in Him; however, I know sometimes in this crazy world we live in that we do have things come up to cause us to worry. So, give your worries up in prayer to God and let Him take care of them because trusting in God and His plan for your life involves casting your cares on Him because He cares for you. Trusting in God's plan will sometimes have you taking steps of faith and knowing that He will guide and provide. Above all, whatever you do to increase your faith and have that unwavering faith and trust in God, stay grounded and anchored in God's Word, the Bible. You will be able to truly see and understand God's character, His promises, and His plan for all of us on this earth. So, by having unwavering faith and trusting the Greater Plan, you will be able to experience God's peace, guidance, and presence in every aspect of your life. So don't let any challenges or difficulties get you down, give them all to God and let Him take care of them in His way and in His time. While you're increasing your faith and getting closer to God, you will notice that the Crown on your heart is standing up straight and shining with the love of Jesus for all to see. Life will have its ups and downs, difficulties, challenges, and heartbreaks yet through it all keep your Crown straight in your heart as you go through life and trust God and have unwavering faith and others will see the love of Jesus shining in all you do!